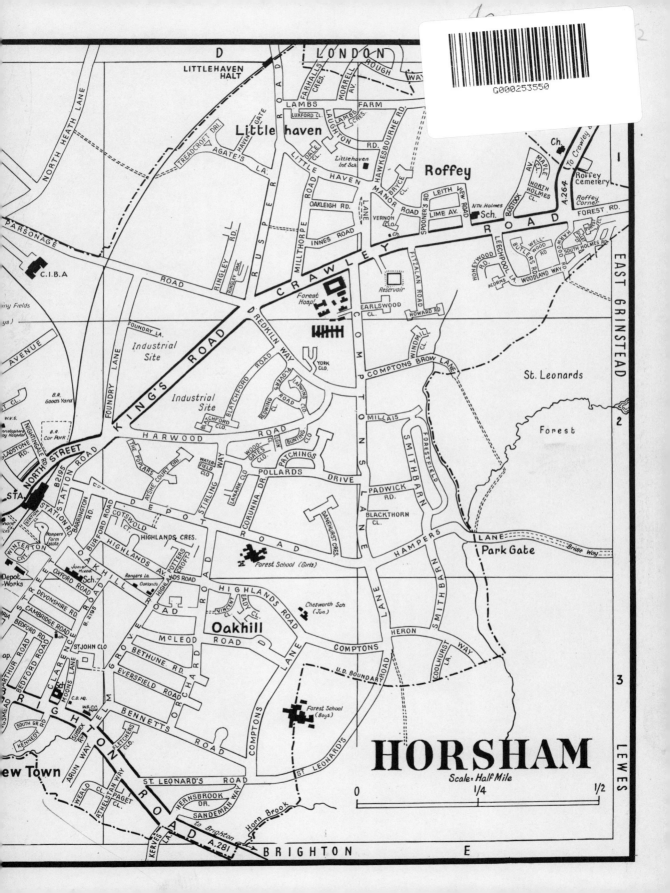

HORSHAM

Scale: Half Mile

0   1/4   1/2

HORSHAM HOUSES

HORSHAM HOUSES

A Study of Early Buildings in a Market Town

Annabelle Hughes

Phillimore

1986

Published by
PHILLIMORE & CO. LTD.,
Shopwyke Hall, Chichester, Sussex

ISBN 0 85033 605 8

Printed and bound in Great Britain by
THE CAMELOT PRESS LTD.
Southampton, England

To those I love, and who care about me

CONTENTS

LIST OF ILLUSTRATIONS

PREFACE

I came to live in Horsham in 1970, and it became clear that this was going to be the first place in which I was ever going to stay long enough to put down a few roots, and to have a sense of belonging. I began to explore the story of the town and of the people who had lived there, delighted that I'd happened upon a place that had a history — and a history that could be pushed back over a thousand years. To get a picture of Horsham from earliest times is rather like having a jigsaw with two-thirds of the pieces missing. The existing third can be laid out to get a rough idea of the shape and colour of the whole, as there are some edge pieces, and diligent searching may turn up part of another third. Small solid areas can be built up, but over a third of the pieces are irretrievably missing, so that the full details of the whole can only be imagined by reference to what *is* there, by intelligent guess-work, and by comparison with information drawn from wider and more complete sources. The process calls for a combination of diligent (and often tedious) research and sheer intuition — a kind of detective mentality — and has the fascination of a 'whodunit' that has no recorded finite solution — a kind of historical Edwin Drood.

It has been like peeling the proverbial onion — layer upon layer, and each one revealing new aspects, different details, suggesting new lines of investigation. In the early days of my searching I was told that 'there is nothing much about Horsham' — but in fact there is a great deal. The information is largely uncollated, mixed up and scattered among a wide range of sources, and apart from Anthony Windrum's *Historical Survey*, no real attempt has been made to unravel the confusion since William Albery's valuable, but often infuriating work in *A Millenium of Facts about Horsham and Sussex* and *Parliamentary History of Horsham*.

This is only an attempt to show how much a study of merely one aspect of Horsham — its early buildings, with documentary support — can contribute to a better understanding of the whole. It is by no means a definitive study, nor a book for specialists, but put forward in the hope that others will follow and extend the work in which I am still involved. On the basis of what has been done to date, several conclusions have been drawn and theories proposed which subsequent finds and research could well prove to be mistaken. The hope is that this record will be a point from which work will proceed, and that at the same time it will give both residents and visitors a greater appreciation of the evidence that still exists of the hundreds of years and lives that have gone to shape the town we see and live in now — a heightened 'sense of place'.

ACKNOWLEDGEMENTS

So many people have given me practical help and encouragement along the way to compiling this book that it is difficult to know where to start with my thanks. The best place, I suppose, is at the beginning, with the buildings, or rather their owners and occupants, who have met my invariable request for 'roof access?' with understanding, and suffered my ferreting around with patience and even enthusiasm, in spite of dusty footprints and disturbed corners. Katherine Morisse persuaded and convinced me that I could take my own photographs, and Arthur and Joan Northcott made it possible for me to do so. Although some of the illustrations in this book are not of a very high standard, they are the only ones available as the buildings have now been demolished. The staff at the West Sussex Record Office and Dr. T. P. Hudson of the Victoria County History have been unfailing sources of help and information. I have 'sat at the feet' of Sylvia Bright, who taught me to measure and draw up houses, and has given freely of her time and knowledge; thanks must also go to Eric, who allows me to take her off at nearly every opportunity, with never a murmur. Finally, I must record how much I appreciate the love and support of my family — parents and children — who have to live with my obsession, to the point that we can no longer eat in the dining room, for all the clutter associated with houses and their history. This is also a small testimony to the value of the years I was married to John, time which gave me the resources to be now as I am.

Annabelle F. Hughes
Horsham
1986

GLOSSARY

aisle
: The space between principal post or arcade post and outside wall, where rafters continue over the eave plate.

bay
: The horizontal distance between one principal post and the next.

barge boards
: Wide board, often moulded or carved, supporting the roof coverings at a gable end and masking the junction between wall and roof.

burgage plot
: A piece of ground within borough boundaries, with or without a house upon it, ownership of which gave the right to vote in borough affairs and for parliamentary members.

burgesses
: Townsmen entitled to vote in borough matters by virtue of ownership of one or more burgage plots.

chantry
: A private chapel or altar with endowments to pay a priest to say memorial masses for an individual or group of individuals.

continuous jetty
: House whose first floor projects over the street along the whole of its length, being floored throughout.

crown-post
: Vertical post, set in the centre of a tie-beam and supporting the collar purlin. It *does not* extend to the ridge, like a king-post.

eave plate
: Longitudinal timber, connecting the principal posts and supporting the rafter ends, on each side of a building.

feet of fines
: Early records of property transactions.

guild, parish
: Corporate body, instituted as a co-operative chantry for the less wealthy parishioners. In Horsham, it also ran a small poor house.

infill
: Any material used to fill the spaces between timbers in a framed building.

inventory
: A list of the moveable assets belonging to an individual, made at the time of death, to help the administration of the will.

collar purlin
: Longitudinal timber supported by crown-posts, which carried the collars that tied together each pair of rafters.

side-purlin
: Longitudinal timber between ridge and eave plate, supporting rafters, and carried by vertical or angled struts set on the ties.

queen strut
: Vertical strut from a principal tie to support side-purlin.

raking strut
: Angled strut from a principal tie to support side-purlin.

sill
: Also known as sole-plate, being the lowest horizontal member of a wall frame, into which posts and studs are tenoned.

subsidy roll
: Early taxation list.

tie-beam, truss
: Horizontal timber between two principal posts.

wattle-and-daub
: Infill made from woven sticks or lathes, plastered with a mixture of clay, dung and chopped straw and lime-washed or painted.

PART ONE

INTRODUCTION

INTRODUCTION

The making of medieval Horsham

BEFORE the Normans arrived in force, the inhabitants of the fertile coastal plain of Sussex had made a habit of driving their animals north into the woodlands of the Weald in the spring and summer, to take advantage of the extra pasturage. They tracked along the river valleys, trod the Roman ways, finding good crossing points and fords, making clearings for summer enclosures and shelters. Some began to stay, building more permanent shelters, beginning to clear and cultivate (assart), or reopen ancient clearings, particularly if they were too poor to own land on the coast. They set up breeding stock — of horses in particular — to serve the needs of travellers, and many of the coastal manors maintained links with 'outliers' in the Weald by continuing to collect tithes and dues from them.

Horsham was on one of the northward tracks, at a good river crossing, and had a special appeal for horse breeders and traders, as the most recent investigations of its name (unchanged since the tenth century) have indicated. It was not far from the well-drained green-sand belt of the Forest of St Leonard, to where the horses could be·moved in winter, so that although they were still near the point of sale and exchange, they were thus saved from being bogged down in the heavy mud by the Arun.

These breeders and traders and their families must have exploited their role in the transport business by bartering and selling other goods and services with their customers. Their success attracted other settlers with different skills, and almost certainly the local thegn provided a wooden church, staffed with a man of his own choice, on the north bank of the river, near the ford. We know the names of two of Horsham's Saxon landowners in the tenth century. Alderman Aethelwold was succeeded by his brother Eadric, when Horsham was still part of the manor of Washington, and the name of one of Horsham's most historic sites — Chesworth — is also Saxon in origin, deriving from 'Ceoldred's worth', 'worth' meaning a land-holding or farm.

When William of Normandy began to consolidate his hold on England, it was of particular importance to secure the south coast against other invaders, and to keep the local people passive. He carved up the area that is now largely Sussex into five strips, running up from the coast in the woodland or Weald.

Each or these strips or rapes was based on a port, and sported a chain of fortified mounds or castles along its north–south line of communication. William de Braose, whom the Domesday survey credits with some 325 manors throughout the south and west, established the principal castle of his rape at Bramber. This was easily accessible by boat from his newly planned port at Shoreham, and was linked with further outposts at Knepp, Sedgwick and Chennelsbrook. It seems too much of a coincidence that these three fortifications are all within a seven mile radius of Horsham — the normal radius for a medieval market was about six and a half miles, to allow for the journey there and back, and trading in between, all within one day.

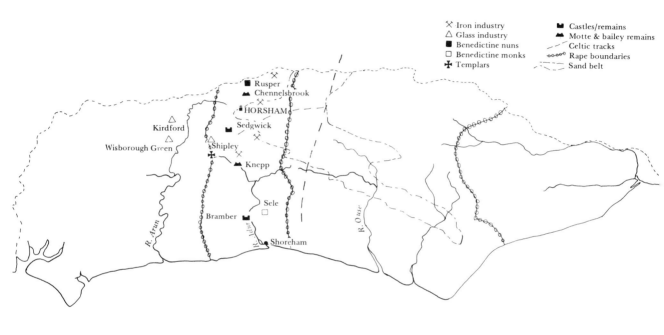

1.   Horsham in its early context.

It seems that not only travellers were making use of what Horsham had to offer in the way of provisions and services, but that those pioneers who were settling in the Weald and beginning to cultivate the wilderness could be sure of being able to buy necessities at the start of their labours, and of finding a ready market when they had something to sell. It was probably William de Braose's son, Philip, who recognised the success and further potential of Horsham when he provided a substantial church building to meet the needs of the growing community, about 1140. Out of the staging post had grown a bustling market centre.

In 1201, the first de Braose's great-grandson, another William, was given a royal charter granting him freedom from royal interference in all his lands. To capitalise on this, and probably in response to local pressure from prospering tenants who wanted more say in their own affairs, he followed the prevailing fashion of the time, and granted Horsham the corporate rights of a borough. In essence, this legally established that the inhabitants of a place could pay rent to their landlord in place of providing labouring services, and that they became a corporate body running their own business. In practice, this was already happening in a number of places where a landowner could make more from rents and market dues than from the labouring services of his tenants, but legal recognition of such status was much sought after. This was certainly so in Horsham by 1235, when it first appears on a document as having borough status. From later records it is clear that regular borough courts were held in the town — the Court Baron, which dealt with matters concerning the ancient customs of the manor and its tenants, the rights of the Lord and the privileges of the tenants; the Court Leet, concerned with the local administration of the borough and dealing with both civil and criminal cases; and the Portmot or Portmoot, which met every three weeks to deal with cases of debt and trespass under 40 shillings. The first two courts were usually presided over by the lord's steward, the latter by locally elected officials.

These officials, chosen from nominees at the Courts Baron and Leet, which were often held together, consisted of one or two bailiffs, two or three constables, a jury of burgesses between 13 and 23 in number, five headboroughs responsible for the several streets, ale conners, leather searchers and sealers, responsible for the measures, weights and qualities of market goods, and a town crier. One or more of these officials are recorded from as early as 1288.

A borough was not only the centre of exchange for the surrounding villages, but also where the country people sent their sons to be bound apprentices to craftsmen and traders. From names on early deeds during the 1200s, we gather that there was a wide range of such men in and around Horsham — drapers, coopers, locksmiths, turners, blacksmiths, hurdle and basket makers, tanners, fullers and taylors, to mention only a few.

It was at this time that the market area must have been officially paced out and the sites for the 52 enfranchised properties established — the burgage plots. These were the plots whose owners paid the corporation's rent to de Braose, who were foremost in the commercial life of the town, and responsible for the borough administration. In Horsham the privileges were attached to certain *sites*, whether open ground or built upon, and not to individuals in their own right. As one would expect, most of the burgages were around the market-place, chosen because it was the nearest largely level space to the river crossing, with a footpath access to the church. It covered all that area now called the Carfax as far down the Causeway as the building that is now the museum — a huge triangle funnelling down to the parish church, which would have functioned as meeting hall, legal centre, and a focus for social activities as well as a place of worship. One or two burgage sites were away from this area, by the older trackway through Horsham to the east. We can imagine that some well-established settlers who had already made their mark in the community and built their homesteads were not to be deprived of their position on the governing body

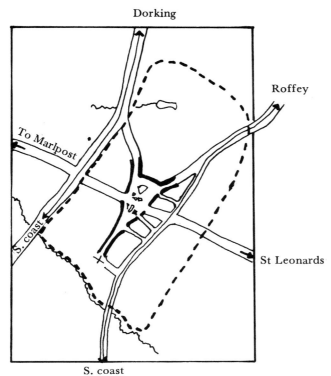

2. Medieval Horsham showing the boundary of the borough (dotted) and the main N/S routes.

just because their houses were not in quite the right place! Thus there were some burgages on Park Street and down into Denne Road.

What had been a rather *ad hoc* business of barter and exchange, functioning on word-of-mouth recommendations and relying chiefly on the travellers whom the terrain compelled through Horsham, now developed into an organised and regulated market economy, taking place on one or two days each week, when the place would seethe with villagers and their produce, animals for sale and slaughter, those pedlars of small wares who wandered from market to market, and the inhabitants of the town making capital out of their week's work. Craftsmen and traders alike operated from the front of their houses, in a room open onto the market place, where those who had travelled in to buy and sell drew up their loaded wagons and carts. As the market became more established and prosperous, shopkeepers erected collapsible counters on their frontages, and travelling traders put up stalls for which they would have been charged ground rent. There were regulations governing the times when these stalls could be put up, and by which they must be dismantled — and traders would be fined for 'forestalling' to try to gain an advantage. Rents were charged to regular stall-holders, and the quality and quantity of certain goods such as bread and ale were maintained by local laws, and sometimes by national legislation, upheld at the manorial and borough courts. The price of bread fluctuated with the price of corn, which was fixed by magistrates after Michaelmas each year, according to the harvest.

Less than thirty years after Horsham had become a borough, the town was such a success that in 1233 the de Braose of the time acquired a grant for a yearly fair, which ran for three days to a week. This attracted people from 20 miles distance, or even farther, and most of these visitors would stay for at least one night, probably paying about a halfpenny for a bed in one of the residents' houses. Tolls were taken on any of the goods brought in, and about threepence a day charged for a stall. A proportion of this income went to the lord of the manor, the rest into the borough's coffers.

'Take-away' food would have been a feature of a fair, in the shape of hot pies and spit-roasted pieces of meat, washed down with weak ale. The ordinary villagers could rub shoulders with wealthy landowners and merchants, even with representatives from the royal household, come to buy provisions for the not-too-distant 'hunting lodges' at Holbrook and Knepp. The town officials were kept constantly on the move, checking weights and measures, collecting dues, hearing complaints and patrolling the fairground at night after curfew. Some fairs operated their own courts to try any cases that arose in the duration — the people of Horsham would have been quite used to such proceedings from their own regular borough courts.

The Assizes at Chichester included several Horsham cases during this period: a wife and her lover killed her husband and fled — they were outlawed; a man killed his brother in a fight; two leading inhabitants were fined for selling wine and cloth against regulations — human nature was not very different, even then!

In 1295, the burgesses of Horsham were summoned to send two representatives to the king's parliament at Westminster. This was not always regarded as a privilege, but often as an onerous duty, to be avoided if possible — the men might have to leave their businesses at an inconvenient time of year, and the town was expected to pay their expenses. On the other hand, it could be an opportunity to make important contacts in a wider sphere of influence for an aspiring local entrepreneur, or landowner. Not all those chosen to represent Horsham in Parliament were as respectable as one might have expected. One of the first men chosen, Walter Randolf, had been one of those who had sold cloth and wine against the assize. We also know that he owned at least four houses, a mill and three acres — a burgage called Randoll's or Randolfes was recorded on the west side of the Carfax as late as 1598. He also owned lands elsewhere in the county. The other man chosen, Walter Burgess, was the founder of the first chantry chapel at the parish church, 13 years later, in 1307. When Burgess died, in 1325, he owned property in the Horsham area worth over £10, and in Warnham, Rusper, Slinfold and Ifield, and of his three daughters, Maud married a Shoreham man, and Alice a man from Winchelsea. Only very wealthy individuals could afford to endow private chantries, and by the early 16th century Horsham parish church contained three private chantries and a parish fraternity chantry for the benefit of the less wealthy. In the documents connected with the first chantry foundation is the first known mention of a commercial premises in the town, as part of the endowment — a shop, rented for 4d. by Alan Dragon — and an Adam Dragon paid tax under 'Rozghee', or Roffey, in 1296.

Even before 1300, the wealth of Horsham can be judged by a very obvious piece of evidence — the parish church. By about 1250, the Norman church had been almost completely replaced by a fine Early English building, with a tall shingled spire added a little later, that would have been visible to travellers approaching from nearly every direction. We know that it was served by at least four clergy. The natural way for a local merchant to demonstrate his success was to put money into the most prestigious local building — the church. Citizens of substance left money for yearly masses or 'obits' for their souls, but the endowment of a chantry with a salaried priest was beyond the means of most. In Horsham, two such chantries were founded, in 1307 and 1447, each with considerable endowments in lands and rents. The signatories and witnesses were men who were high on the subsidy lists, and who represented Horsham themselves, or came from families that did so. Moreover, in 1457, a parish guild or 'brotherhood' was set up as a kind of co-operative chantry for those who were not

---

Horsham Burgesses recorded in the taxations of 1296, 1327 and 1332

Walt. Randolf*	Jn. le Boteler*	Jn. Butelir*
Rich. Neel	Mich. Aside [? aLyde]	Galf. le Fisher
Id. Relicta Chauntrel	Will. Gosseling	Jn. atte Lynde
Galf. le Boteler	Rico. atte Stanstrete*	Mich. aLyde
Walt. le Borgeys*	Jn. Clymping	Ric. le Pyk
Rado atte Stanstrete*	Alic. le Turnour	Will. Gosselyn
Matild. Relicta Maresch.	Galf. le Fyssher	Jn. Laurens
Jn. Pecoc maior	Rob. le Stupere	Jn. le Baker
Rob. le Cradel	Pet. le Turnour	Will. le Tourneur
Mart. le Peec*	Matill. atte Boure	Pet. le Tourneur*
Rich. le Hert	Laur. le Baker	Jn. le Budel
Nich. atte Rydeforde	Nich. Fabro	God. le Boghier
Will. le Coupe	Jn. atte Lynde	Matild. atte Boure
Will. Wardhech	Will. Stedman	Lucya atte Brome
Will. le Chalener	Ad. Quillard	Will. le Digher
Rob. Godfray*	Thom. le Bakere	Jn. Godefray*
Thom. Bibon	Will. Bochier	Thom. le Glovar*
Rd. Conky	Thom. le Glover*	Walt. Randekyn*
Ad. Cotsyn	Oliver Skilling*	Ric. atte Stanstret*
Pet. atte Linde	Will. Turnour	Oliver Skylling*
Sim. atte Moure	Alic. atte Brome	Laurens le Baker
Rich. le Tournur	Will. le Chalner	Rob. le Stupere
Rich. le Wuchere	Jn. Cole	Nich. Fabro
Rand. de Horsham*	Will. le Dygher	Jn. Marchaunt*
Jn. atte Lynde	Math. Godelove	Jn. Nel*
Morgan Hugon	Jn. Marchaunt	Ad. Quillard
Will. le Rideler	Ric. le Pek	
Will. le Saltere	Rog. Randolf	
Rob. atte Welle	Jn. Godefrai	
Rob. de Horleye	God. Quillard	
Rob. le Mareschal	Ric. Whychere	
Will. Godeman	Jn. le Bonwyck	
Gilb. atte Boure	Ric. Burgeis	
Ben. Bockhorn	Nich. Swenge	
Pho. Craddoc	Rog. le Singar	
Will. Elrich		
Galf. Handhamer		
Jn. Mohe		
Jn. Pecoc minor		
Will. le Skinnere		
Jn. le Skinnere		
Will Waryn		

These lists are presented in order of wealth, calculated on their *borough* possessions — several owned lands elsewhere. It is interesting to notice the recurring family names, and those that give a clue to the man's calling, or are descriptive. *Indicates that he represented the borough at least once at a parliament.

rich enough to pay for their own, and also to run a small poor house for the really destitute, near the west end of the church, in the Normandy. Photographs of this building, and of the 'priests' house' — perhaps associated with one or other of the chantries — have been identified. We know that by the early 15th century there was a beautifully carved chancel screen, painted with the twelve apostles, surmounted by a beam carrying a rood — a crucifixion scene — and in the choir was a painted statue of the pieta — the Virgin Mary with the body of her Son in her arms. The painted wooden ceiling and angel-figures may also have originated at this time, although they have been restored and retouched since.

From the end of the 13th century, events continue to underline the importance of Horsham, not only in the local economy, but in a wider context, making it a desirable place to settle, build, expand and consolidate. In 1306, the assizes came to town for the first time, and from then on Horsham acted as host in turn with Lewes and Chichester. To have some idea of the impact of such an event, the assizes that year dealt with 36 civil cases, 22 criminal cases, and 21 pleas of complaint, mostly concerning trespass and assault. Imagine how many days it must have taken to get through all that business, and the number of people who were involved — the justices, their retinues and officials, the accused, their witnesses and accusers, witnesses for the prosecution and various juries drawn from local communities — not to mention any 'hangers-on'. These people would have required food and lodging for the duration, and probably almost doubled the population of the borough. County coroners also began holding court in Horsham about this time, to conduct the investigations and procedure connected with the discovery of dead bodies. Two coroners were penalised for failing to turn up in Horsham in 1321.

Among the representatives that Horsham continued to send to Parliaments — held not only at Westminster, but also at York, Salisbury, Gloucester and Winchester — were men called le Gretesmyth, le Flechiere, Cok, le Barbour, Nywebakere, Spicer and Jewdry. The subsidy returns contain many other names indicating occupations, such as glover, merchant, wool beater, flagon-maker, as well as butcher, baker and dyer. Horsham's wealth and prosperity depended on the success of her traders, their contacts and influences. Even thieves recognised this, like the three who were indicted at Guildford assizes in 1315, for 'robbing certain foreign merchants outside Horsham to the west' of goods to the value of £40! One of the earliest maps of Britain is called the Gough Map and dates from 1350. It includes many, if not most of the places that stood on main roads, and shows a national network of roads radiating from the capital. Among the number of short-distance routes from London to the Channel ports is that running via Dorking and Horsham to Shoreham, so Horsham was already on a 'recommended' travellers' route. In 1350, the City of London Corporation wrote to Horsham about a complaint they had received that the bailiffs of Horsham had taken matters into their own hands to try to prevent traders in livestock by-passing the town, presumably for higher prices — they had arrested some Farnham men who had bought such cattle and wrested a promise from them that they would do so no more!

During the first 150 years or so of parliamentary representation, the town's MPs do appear to have been genuinely resident, and thoroughly involved in all that was going on locally. They seem to have been drawn from the traders and craftsmen upon whom the town's prosperity had been built. Not all were upright members of society untouched by scandal, as we have already seen. Walter Randekyn first appears on the subsidy roll of 1332 as a burgess, and subsequently, in about 1333, he was accused of taking £20 worth of wine, being involved with wreckers at Worthing, trespassing, poaching and assaulting servants all on the lands of John de Mowbray. When his wife Alice died in 1351, he did undertake to give 6s. 8d. to the poor of Horsham for 20 years — conscience money? He represented Horsham seven times from 1337, and was succeeded by his son — another Walter — who also went to parliaments seven times. Walter the father was murdered in 1357, and although his servant, Joan atte Naldrette, was indicted for being party to and aiding the felony, she was granted a royal pardon, apparently because she was able to prove her innocence. Walter the son was also a county coroner in 1390, but he was no worthier than his father, for he was called to account with John Bradbrugge the younger, bailiff of Bramber rape, for a conspiracy to defraud, over legal fines, whereby they both received a share.

Roger Elyot, who represented Horsham in 1421, was described as a 'chapman' of Horsham — a seller of small wares — when he was indicted for two hanging offences some six years apart. It was said that in 1429, he had broken into John Dawtre's house in Horsham, assaulted his wife, Pernell, and taken a 'maser' or cup worth 6s. 8d., a silver girdle worth 20s., and three gowns worth 40s. Furthermore, that in 1435, he had broken into the Southwark home of Sir Hugh Halsham, smashed open a chest with an iron bar, and stolen two furred garments worth 10 marks (a mark was about 13s. 4d.). However, during the trial, it appeared that one of the jurors, Stephen Sloughterforth of Warnham, was himself under suspicion, and Roger too received a royal pardon, although one feels that there was more to this case than meets the eye. Even the more humble residents of Horsham were temptation enough to a thief. Henry Reperose, who had a 'close and buildings' in 1456, had two yards of blanket, a doublet and a yard of kersey to the value of 4s. stolen from him, by Thomas Cornewayll, a carpenter of Lewes.

By 1500, Horsham not only had its own twice-weekly market and yearly fair, and played host to both coroners' courts and assizes, but the Archbishop of Canterbury had been allowed a charter — in 1449 — for a weekly market and two fairs, to be held in his outlier of Marlpost, which included the area now called the Bishopric. Presumably this was to capitalise on the prosperity of the adjoining town, and it is possible that what is now the *Green Dragon* public house, where 18th-century manorial courts were held, was even then a centre of administration, and maybe even the dwelling for the beadle of Marlpost.

Houses in medieval Horsham

The earliest description of a dwelling near Horsham that I have found comes from the Chartulary of Sele Priory, near Beeding, and refers to a property in the Forest of St Leonard in 1285:

all the buildings of that tenement well thatched and protected and well enclosed with wooden
walls for the most part and with earthen walls round . . .

A fictionalised, though informed picture of a house in its early Sussex setting appears
in Alfred Duggan's *Knight with Armour*, imagined in the year 1096:

> Conversation was impossible on the ride, as the horses struggled in single file, girth-deep
> in the muddy clay track, through the deep tangled woods of the Weald; but in the evening
> they crossed the river and rode up the hill to the timber-and-wattle hall that looked north-
> wards to the endless woods of Kent.

Today we are most familiar with the idea of building from some kinds of blocks
and mortar, relying on the force of gravity to hold the whole thing together. Early
houses in Horsham, as in the rest of the country, were built from the materials that
came easily to hand — in this case this meant timber, straw, sticks, animal hair, mud,
and later, split stone. This is what is meant by the term 'vernacular architecture'
— dwellings built from easily-available local materials. Houses like the forest tenement
needed frequent renewal, and none have survived except as traces found in archaeological excavations. Timber-framed buildings, largely prefabricated as open wooden
frames, sometimes at a distance from the actual site, sometimes at an on-site saw-pit
dug for the purpose, relied on oak-pegged joints to keep them together, and 'gave'
to survive harsh weather or ground settlement. Once jointed together, a giant hand

3. Houses like the forest tenement needed frequent renewal, and none have survived, except as traces
found in archaeological excavations. (Reconstruction from archaeological evidence: Weald and Down-
land Museum, Singleton).

4. Once jointed together, a giant hand could have picked one up, turned it around, and put it down again, without any great disturbance to its basic structure. (Chilsfold Farm, Northchapel).

could have picked one up, turned it around, and put it down again, without any great disturbance to its basic structure. It was quite accepted that the wattle-and-daub infill which complemented the flexibility of the framing would need periodic patching or replacement.

The earliest houses would have been one-room constructions, open to the rafters, with a central fire on a stone hearth, and the householders had to be very good at slow-burning dry wood, and possibly charcoal, to get the maximum heat for the longest time with the minimum smoke. We must be careful not to exaggerate the smallness and wretchedness of these early houses. In the court rolls for 1281 of Halesowen, Worcestershire, the specifications of a house are given. It was to be the 'dower' house for the mother of a man who was taking over her land on her retirement, and it was 30 feet long between the end walls, and 14 feet wide, with corner posts, three new doors and two windows — an early 'granny wing'. The main house on the holding must have been larger still. In order to gain some privacy in these open-hall houses, the roof sometimes extended beyond the eaves to form side-aisles, and hangings between the aisle posts then created some kind of screened-off area. The number of different words used for houses in early records, such as the Domesday Book, suggest that there were various traditional kinds of houses, different both in plan and size. However, while life was still comparatively harsh and basic, governed by sunrise and sunset, and revolving around the seasons and the demands of land and animals, this open, communal pattern of living continued.

As communities became more organised, and a social structure began to emerge that was more than just peasant and lord, there was a greater demand for privacy among lesser men, who required houses that could fulfil more sophisticated functions, which had a greater degree of comfort and convenience. Screens were inserted to divide off the 'service' areas from the main living area, and floors were put in at the ends of houses to capitalise on space, and to provide private apartments for the master of the house and his family. In some cases existing houses were adapted to meet these needs, in others new houses were purpose-built in new styles. The documentary evidence for houses in Horsham before 1300 is rather scarce. Almost all the references are in the 'Feet of Fines' — a kind of registry of property deals — and there are about a dozen of these between 1236 and 1300. Several houses are mentioned briefly in the Chartulary of Sele over a similar period, and the vicar's manse is recorded in 1231. There is only one house in the Horsham area, beyond the town, that can possibly be placed within this period on stylistic evidence, and then only a portion of it — and this is Chennelsbrook, on the Rusper road, which was an aisled hall. This has probably survived because it was out in the country, and of superior build, as it had connections with the de Braose family and possibly supplanted the earlier motte-and-bailey fortification to the north.

Over the next hundred years about 40 properties feature in the Feet of Fines and other documents, including five shops and a mill, including the following examples:

In 1305, Nicholas atte Redforde and his wife settled a house and six acres on their daughter, Matilda, who had married a Richard Morgan (a name indicating Welsh origin at a time when names were still descriptive). A Hugh Morgan paid tax as a burgess in 1296. In the same year Nicholas and his wife also settled a house on their son, John.

In 1318, a house and 30 acres went to William, son of William de Assheleye, for £20; in 1330 and 1334, houses went for 100 shillings.

In 1345, a house and 3 roods cost £10, and in the following year, Peter and Isabella le Tournor rented a house and 3 acres for 9 shillings and a rose at Midsummer. ('A rose at Midsummer' features in several of the records, perhaps as a traditional sign of good faith.)

In 1362, grants of tenements were made on 'the highway from the market-place to Guildford', and 'the highway from the market-place to St Leonard's', indicating that the lines of East and West Streets were well established by that time.

In 1367, John Borle let 2 houses, 2 shops and their land for 2s. 6¾d. to John and Emma Hadresham, and Thomas and Alice Chamberleyn.

In 1369, in a deal between Roger Bushop and Thomas Jewary, the property is described thus: 'Shop, with an upper story (or loft) built thereon, in Horsham,

which the said Roger once granted for the life of the said Thomas, abutting S
on a tenement of said Thomas beside Horsham market place, W on a shop of
John Basch'.

It is clear that by the early 14th century there were permanent retail premises in
Horsham, and by the latter part of the century it is very probable that some of these
may have been encroachments onto the original open market-place — weekly stalls
turned permanent shops. Evidences of early buildings in the Middle Street area make
it not unreasonable to imagine that this was one of Horsham's earliest 'shopping
precincts' developed out of the temporary market stalls that began to remain from
one market to the next, and then became increasingly more and more substantial. As
late as the 18th century, this was still known as Butchers' Row, so it is tempting to
imagine it as a medieval 'shambles', the narrow alleys remaining to remind us of the
passages between the stalls.

These narrow alleys or 'twittens' that even re-building has preserved, or in some
cases imitated, are a feature of modern Horsham that medieval residents would find
familiar. The routes along Pirie's Alley, Talbot or Pump Alley, Colletts Alley, the lanes
on each side of the large store in Middle Street (once Grants and earlier, Chart's) were
all laid down early in the town's history, as examination of the buildings in their
immediate vicinity has supported. There were very likely others of which only vestiges
remain, for instance by the side of the Pipe Shop in Middle Street, and each side of the
block that recently contained Weller Eggar, on the eastern side of the Carfax. The
Swan Walk complex is just a modern interpretation of a similar theme. In some cases
these lanes were established as early access to the 'backsides' of properties, where
residents remained in touch with their recent agricultural roots, tending orchards,
growing vegetables and hops, and keeping livestock such as pigs and goats, ducks, geese
and chickens. In others, as the market-place was slowly eroded by more permanent
buildings, the lanes between are a reminder of the ways between different stalls and
'speciality' areas — livestock and butchery, small wares and pedlary, drapery and enter-
tainment. In two cases they seem to be the remains of the old links between the
'main road' through Horsham — Park Street/Denne Road or Back Lane/Friday Street
as it was once called — and the new market-place. In a way, even East Street can be
regarded as a twitten 'grown large'.

Although in any town there must have been constant re-building and expanding,
medieval demolitions did not usually involve a bonfire. Anyone who has spent time
looking over timber-framed buildings will very quickly realise that in a 'hand-made'
world, ready-prepared timbers were never wasted but re-used wherever possible.
Empty mortices and peg-holes in apparently unnecessary places are calculated to add
to the problems and fascination of interpreting early houses. (The term 'ships' timbers',
however, has found a far more sensible interpretation of late: it probably applied to
timber of a particular quality, just as we speak of 'marine ply'.) In the rolls of the
manor of Wiston, near Steyning, for 1357, there is a detailed record of what happened
to one house in Horsham, when it seemed to become surplus to requirements, perhaps

as a result of the Black Death which had rampaged through England between 1347 and 1350. The house was bought for 66s. 9d., the stone roof dismantled and carted down to Steyning at the cost of 6s. 10d. for a repair job, and the timber sold off in Horsham for 16s. 8d. (The average weekly wage for a building labourer at about that time was roughly two shillings.)

The influence of some families over several generations can be traced through such records, and is reflected in property deals. There were the Butlers, who must have been the original owners of the burgage plot of that name in North Street, adjacent to and part of the earliest Horsham gaol; Galfrid le Boteler was a witness to the endowment of the Holy Trinity chantry in 1307, and was well-to-do on the evidence of the first tax assessment of 1296. John Butiler figures high on the next two subsidies, of 1327 and 1332, and the family represented Horsham at parliaments over a span of 58 years. The chantry of 1447 was set up to the memory of Henry Botiler and his wife, by Richard Wakehurst, the county member, and others. In 1423, Henry Frenssh left a missal, chalice and vestments to the Holy Trinity chantry, as well as 20 pence for the parish clerk, who was probably living in part of what is now 'Minstrels' in the Causeway — the traditional home of the parish clerk. Frensshes had been MPs 12 times during the 14th century, and the 1611 Borough survey mentions a tenement called 'the Red Lion, formerly Frensshes' on the corner of West Street and Carfax, where Chart and Lawrence now stands. In a 1612 *inquisition post mortem*, the *Red Lion*, which was then in the Tredcroft family, is described as having a hall, chamber, parlour and little parlour on the ground floor, a little chamber 'at the stayers head', four chambers on the first floor including 'Old Bottinges chamber', and three garrets, apart from the usual offices — kitchen, buttery, bakehouse, brew-house and all with lofts — and cellars. The original building must have been considerably expanded over the centuries, or it may have been a late 15th-century re-build. The Botting family can be linked, in turn, with the house on the burgage plot opposite Sun Alliance in North Street, known in the late 16th century as 'The George, formerly Bottings', and they included a shoemaker and two butchers at about that time. The Tredcrofts appear to have moved to Horsham from Billingshurst in the late 16th century, when Thomas Tredcroft, dying in 1564, is recorded as 'a tailor, of Horsham'. His son, Robert, was a vintner, who owned the *Red Lion*, the grandson, another Robert, supplied wine for the church communions, and *his* son, Nathaniel, who may have acquired 15–16 the Causeway after the death of Hall Ravenscroft in 1681, was not only rated as the wealthiest man in Horsham, but was also presented by Cromwell as its vicar.

In 1430, the junction of Denne Road and East Street was called Stanestreet cross, and Richard atte Stanestret is mentioned in many early documents as a wealthy burgess, property owner and MP over 21 years. On the corner of Denne Road is one of Horsham's most impressive early houses, now in two ownerships as newsagents and a restaurant, and known variously as Bishop's and Grace's in records from the 17th century. It is one of the town's characteristic well-to-do medieval houses, with a central hall some 20 feet wide between two cross-wings.

The next documentary milestone for Horsham is the subsidy for 1524-5 when the property owners and residents were listed by street — North, South (Causeway), East and West Streets, and The Skarfolks. A list of those in the Marlpost area, which included the Bishopric and Worthing Road area, is given for the same period.

SUBSIDY ROLLS, 1524-5

1524 — MARLEPOSTE

Thomas Trowar	..	..		4			John Ingram	..	..		20
Thomas Holbroke		..		20			Wyllyam Pancras		..		20
Walter Skynner	..	..		10			Thomas S.	..	..		...
Thomas Wales	..	..		6	13	4	John Fraunces, Frenchman[1]				...
*Rychard Ford	..	..		6	13	4	John Gatland, servant to				
John Barkar	..	..		6	13	4	John Barker[1]	..			...
Wyllyam [On]sty	..	L	4	13	4		John Hurrok	..	..	D	1
*Thomas Heyleyng		..		2			Robert Dorant	..		D	1
Nycholas Grenyar		..		6	13	4	John Weller	..	..	D	1
Nele M...a	..	..		...			John Davy	..	..	D	1
John Pylfold	..	..		20			*Rychard Warde		..	D	1
Rychard Fust	..	..		2			John Hatchett	..		D	1
Wyllyam Pylfold	..	..		30			Robert Wattes	..		D	1
Harry Pylfold	..	..		3			Wyllyam Bocher		..	D	1
Thomas Bocher	..	..		2			*Rychard Master		..	D	1
Thomas Sayars	..	..		5			Thomas Sylkden		..	D	1
Symon Fuller	..	..		2			John Fraunces, a Fracheman,				
Thomas Jope	..	..		5			seruant to Wyllyam Waller			A	2
Thomas Pylfold	..	..		20			(in the arte of tanning)				
Rychard Stydolf	..	..		20							

Sum £9 12s. 2d.

1525

Nicholas Monary	..	..		5		Wyllyam Stydolf		..	A	2

Sum £9 10s. 8d.

Subcollectors Rychard Stydolf & Wyllyam Pancras

Sum total for the Liberty (and half-hundred), 1524, £19 13s. 6d., 1525, £25 10s. 10d.

THE BOROUGH OF HORSHAM

1524 — THE EST STRETE

John Dungate	..	..		2			Rychard Ryvhow hys seruant	A	1
Robert Rychardson		..		5			Andrew Robynson	..		4
Edward Terell	..	..		3			Rychard Froyle	..		6
Rychard Ive	..	..		13	6	8	*John Dykynson	..	D	1
Rychard Sowten	..	..		6	13	4	*Rychard a Wode	..	D	1
John Wykyn	..	..	L	5			Nicholas Smalpece	..	D	1
John Bokar	..	..		2	13	4	*Bartylmew Thurstyll	..	D	1
Robert Bokar	..	..		26	13	4	Henry Owton	..	D	1
Henry Fylpott	..	..		2			John Gylle(t), Frensheman	D	1
George Repkyn	..	..	L	3			Rychard Warde	..	D	1
John Gamyll, pynner	..		3			Rychard Jakett	..	D	1
*John Swan hys seruant	..	A	1			Thomas Roser	..	D	1

1525

Hamlett Pynnar	..	..	D	1	John Owten	..	..	D	1
John Froyle	..	..	D	1				

1524 — THE WESTRETE

Name	Code	£	s	d	Name	Code	£	s	d
Jamys Monyar		3	6	8	*Henry Baker	x	1	6	8
Nycholas Hurst		40			Wyllyam Hynde	x	1	6	8
John Saltos hys seruant	A	2			Rychard Starr	x	1	6	8
Roger Oswy		2			John Sowter	x	1		
Rychard Ive, junior		2			Thomas Mylward	x	1		
Thomas Cok		2			John [We]ller, shomaker	x	1		
Wyllyam Page		2			Thomas Amys	x	1		
John Jenyn		2			*Rychard Burndysch	x	1		

1525

Name	Code	£	Name	Code	£
William Hynde		1	Thomas Aylesbury	D	1
Richard Starr		1	Anne Dalton	D	1
John Goldyng	D	1			

1524 — THE NORTHSTRETE

Name	Code	£	s	d	Name	Code	£	s	d
Emery Tusman		6	13	4	†Wyllyam Prest hys seruant	A	2		
John Alyson[1]		6	13	4	John Rychardson	A	1		
Henry Bull		2			*Robert Carpenter	A	1		
Rychard Bone		2			Richard Alyngham	A	1		
Thomas Wuller		2			*Rychard Robert	A	1		
Margery Wodsyll		20			*Thomas Clarke	A	1		
John Bottyng		2			*Henry Tully	A	1		
Thomas Barnefeld		2			John Long	D	1		
John Bedyll		26	13	4	Edward Bassett	D	1		

1525

Name	Code	£	Name	Code	£
William Prest, John Bedyll's servant	G	2	John Rychardson	D	1
			Richard Alyngham	D	1

[1] Alynson in 1525

1524 — THE SOUTHSTRETE

Name	Code	£	s	d	Name	Code	£	s	d
[a]Auery Bartwyke Esquier and ys decayed sins the lone by the reason that he hath graunted the offyce of the controllership of the porte of Chichester to Thomas Awcokk and also ys decayed further of iiij[or] markes in londes that he hath gevyn to Eleynore hussay hys doughter in law	L F	54	6	8	Henry Mychell		20		
					Jone Lede (widow)		2		
					Wyllyam Onsty		2		
					Roger Alen		6		
					John Wuller		4		
					*John Glover hys seruant	A	1		
					Thomas Lyntott		2		
					John Newman		3		
					*John Hadman		2		
					*John Storer		40		
					Rychard Skynnar		2		
[a]Edmond Says		53	6	8	The londes of the Fraternyte of Seynt John & Seynt				
[a]Elyzabeth Foys and ys decayed ix[li] sins the lone by the deth of Rychard Grover of Godyl-myng whych ys deceased & left nothyng to pay hys dettes and also ys ferther decayed v[li] by the deth of one Rafe Furber of Shore-ham whych ys deceased & left nothing		53	6	8	Anne in yerely value	L	8		
					*Rychard Grenyar	x	1		
					Edward Alderton	x	1		
					Henry Cadman	x	1		
					*Robert Heywode	x	1		
					Robert Gorynge	x	1	6	8
					Robert Stroger	x	1		
					Raynold Myles	x	1		
					*Nicholas Grenyar	x	1		
					Rychard Brandon	x	1		
					*John Thomas	x	1		

Harry Foys	..	..		26	13	4	Thomas Harryson	..		x	1	
Wyllyam Pudon	..	..		10			Rychard Mornsale	..		x	1	
John Rose				2			Thomas Mylys	..		x	1	
Wyllyam Danyell	..	..		6	13	4						

1525

John Hurst	..	..	L	2	William Waterman	..	D	1
Edward Holond	..	..	D	1	Thomas a Dene	..	D	1
Thomas Molyng	..	..	D	1	Thomas Wryght	..	D	1
Thomas Saunder	..	..	D	1				

1524   THE SKARFOLKES

Rychard Busshop	..		30			Rychard Sharpe	..		20		
John Alyn, mercer	..		6			John a Godyshalf	..		6	13	4
John Capelen	..	..	10			*Rychard Turnor	..	x	1		
Thomas Elys	..	..	16	13	4	Wyllyam Smalham	..	x	1		
Rychard Warde	..	..	6	13	4	Rychard Barwyke	..	x	1		
Thomas Sandsale	..	x	1			Rychard Roser	..	x	1		
*Wyllyam Gate	..	x	1			John Snellyng	..	..	x	1		
*John Tully	..	..	x	1		*Thomas Rydrede	..	x	1		
Wyllyam Barowe	..	x	1			*Olyver Wyllyams	..	x	1		

1525

John Aylwerde	..	..	2	John Tely	..	..	D	1
Henry Snellyng	..	..	2	Thomas Rode	..	D	1
Thomas Herdyng	..	..	2	Nycholas Sharpe	..	D	1
John Turnor	..	..	D	1				

Sum, 1524, £27 16s. 8d.; *Subcollectors (illegible)*

1525, £27 5s. 2d.; *Subcollectors* John Wullar & John Bokar

NOTE — *No basis of assessment is given for many persons in Horsham assessed at £1 and £1 6s. 8d.; these are shown by the 1525 list to be taxed on wages.*

As a general rule, only about 70 per cent. of the population were liable for tax, the rest being too poor, and even then tax evasion was not unknown! Of the 127 people rated for tax in the borough, five were wealthy, 11 middle-class, 39 lower middle-class and 79 employed working class: this is judging purely on financial criteria. Among the most comfortably-off were some well-established Horsham families — the Foys (Voices), Hursts, Michells, and Pilfolds (in Marlpost). Although four out of the five wealthiest lived in South Street, the rest of the residents were fairly evenly distributed through the town, and many of those taxed at lower assessments were obviously servants or employees. A tailor, butcher and shoemaker were among the middle-class — two of them living in the Skarfolks, where a mercer and a weaver also lived. It is not too fanciful to imagine someone like Richard Busshop, who was taxed on £30, living in a house in the centre of the Carfax, where the remains of a high-class cross-wing house can be found in the present K Shoe Shop. Thomas Elys, a butcher, may well have carried on his business in one of the buildings we know to have existed on both sides of Middle Street, formerly Butchers' Row. Perhaps he traded out of the building that stood on the present site of Robert Dyas, which has been identified as one or two shops with shuttered counters; or from part of the long range that borders Colletts Alley, with its barn-like back stores. The existence of these pre-1520 properties implies the existence of other buildings as old, if not older, as side walls of one always butted up to other buildings, and the southern end of the other had been demolished and replaced in the early 16th century.

The Wealden house which stands almost intact on the eastern side of the Carfax next to Pirie's Alley, could have housed a man like John Alyn, mercer, who was almost certainly the father of the twins Matthew and James — the first of whom became vicar of Horsham, the latter master of Collyer's Free School. This building was large enough to have housed both a large family and a business, and was one of several on a burgage plot called the Chequer. On the opposite side of the Carfax were not only a fine house, later known as Bornes, fit to house someone like Richard Sharpe, a tailor, but also a more humble dwelling, part of which appears in an early photograph, and was perhaps more suited to a weaver or fletcher, or may even have been divided into one-room tenements for some of the poorer workmen.

At this time William Daniel was the parish clerk, living in a house near to the churchyard, cheek by jowl with such exalted people as Avery Bartwyke — once controller of the port of Chichester — and Horsham MP Edmond Says (who with Bartwyke was one of the commissioners for the subsidy) as well as Elisabeth and Harry Foys, widow and second son of that Richard who died in 1513, and who was later remembered with his wife in monumental brasses in the church. (Only Elisabeth's still remains.) The Foys possibly lived on the site of what is now the RSPCA headquarters, which was part of the manor of Hewells. Harry's eldest daughter, another Elisabeth, was to marry Richard, the son of Richard Busshop or Bishop of the Skarfolkes, in 1541. Widowed in 1554, she appears to have strayed from the straight and narrow, for she subsequently bore two bastards to Thomas Bradbridge, the Bradbridges being another family of some local standing. Her mother and sister-in-law, by contrast, had both re-married to members of the household of the Earl and Countess of Arundel, who would probably have visited at Chesworth, the home of the dowager Duchess of Norfolk. The Bishops were probably also connected with that burgage at the top of Denne Road, and the marriage between Richard and Elisabeth is only one example of the many such alliances — most probably 'arranged' — that went on between leading Horsham families, the settlements nearly always involving land and property.

Neither East Street nor West Street contained burgage properties, originating as they had out of the tracks that linked the market place with St Leonards and Marlpost. Nevertheless, several of the owners and/or residents in those streets were well-off, according to the 1524-5 subsidy. Richard Ive lived in East Street, and owned a property in West Street which was tenanted by his son, Richard, a shoemaker. The property formerly Leach's fishmongers is the cross-wing to a larger house, and had a hall to the east, of which a small portion remains, and there was possibly an eastern cross-wing too. A pinner, two fullers and a glover also lived, and probably traded, in East Street, all being connected with the clothing trade. John Gamyll, the pinner, was prosperous enough to have two of his servants — John Swan and Richard Ryvhow — recorded for taxation. Other records and photographs indicate at least two other houses, possibly of medieval origin, and certainly timber-framed.

John Jenyn, who is on the 1524–5 subsidy list, lived in West Street, and from other sources we know that he was a 'surgeon' and lived in a house called Grenehurst. This could well have been that small, three-bay house that was demolished in the 1960s to make way for the modern block which contains the gas showrooms — also three-bay! Who was then living in the *Red Lion*, we are not quite sure, although Nicholas Hurst, the smith, was rated at £40, and was living in a house called Haynes, owned by a Michell. He had at least one servant, and when he died in 1534, left three anvils and other tools to his son Richard, as well as three other houses and lands, and yet another 'little house called Harpers' to his daughter Jane. It was a descendant of his, Robert, who was described as a tailor in 1703, when he bought Bolters — 15–16 Causeway — from the son of the wealthy vicar of Horsham, another Nathaniel Tredcroft.

By the 17th century the heyday of timber-framed building was past, although the town possesses one or two fine examples of post-medieval houses built in the last flourish of the tradition by contemporary men of substance. The front range of Bolters, and of the Museum, 11, Market Square, and the building on the corner of North Street and Carfax — all these would have presented the overhanging jettied fronts and close-timbering that are most familiar to the general public as 'Elizabethan' or 'Jacobean'. In other cases down East Street, and probably West Street, spaces that had been cultivated land or garden 'closes' were filled in with a rash of buildings which sometimes re-used old timbers, were often built to be plastered over or in-filled with brick, and whose timbers were often less than impressive because they were not intended to show. That the townspeople were still prosperous traders is demonstrated by the history of its free school — Collyer's — and in the move to more 'modern' styles of building, presaged by Mr. Tredcroft's house of 1703, the core of the Manor House, Causeway, and the replacement of the timber-framed building on the Cockmans burgage site, now Park House.

How timber-framed buildings hold together

A timber-framed building is constructed, as the name indicates, from a number of wooden frames. What started as a simple open-work box, the spaces filled in with woven sticks plastered over with mud and straw or hair, developed into a series of boxes, some set at right angles to each other, some sharing a side with the adjacent box.

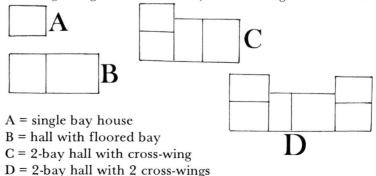

A = single bay house
B = hall with floored bay
C = 2-bay hall with cross-wing
D = 2-bay hall with 2 cross-wings

The corner posts of each box were set into a base frame or *sill*, resting on the ground, that ran all the way around the bottom of the house. The sill itself was sometimes underpinned with stone or rubble. The space between each pair of posts is called a *bay*.

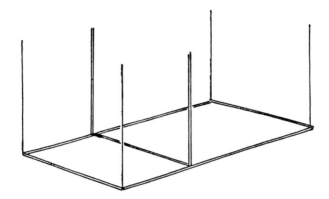

Each pair of principal posts were fastened together at the top with a *tie-beam*.

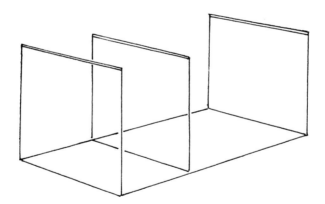

An *eave-plate* joined principal posts along each side.

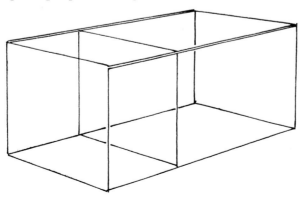

A *crown-post* was set upon the middle of each tie-beam, braced down to the ties at the ends of the building.

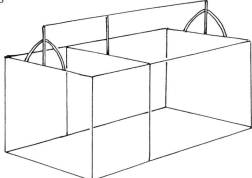

These crown-posts supported a *purlin* which ran the length of the building, and were braced up to it.

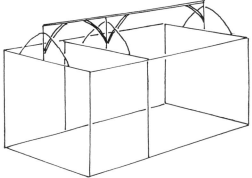

Across the purlin were set the short *collars* which held together each pair of rafters.

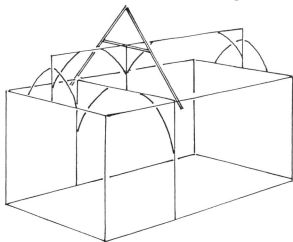

The principal timbers were tied together with a framework of short timbers, set vertically, horizontally, and sometimes diagonally, to provide extra bracing strength. Windows and doors could be included within this framework. All the timbers were held together by a combination of tenons, mortices, joints and oak pegs.

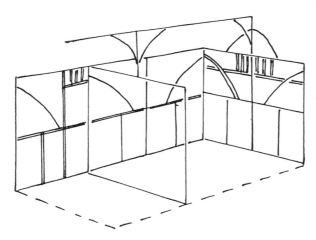

Of course, this does not give the *sequence* of construction, as most of the framework was assembled on the ground in units and then hauled into place — I have just tried to show the *relationship* between the different parts of such a house.

Vertical stakes were then set into the spaces in the framework, and thin sticks or split oak laths woven between them, as with hurdles or wattle fencing. A daub of mud, often mixed with straw or hair, covered it over, and the whole would be lime-washed, frame and all, to give a degree of protection against fire.

The house could then be roofed with thatch, tiles, or more often in the Horsham area with local stone, sliced into slabs, and set with the largest at eave level, diminishing in size to the ridge. Though soft when quarried, local stone hardens when exposed. To carry a stone roof the rafters needed to be substantial, and to be set at not less than a 45° angle, often much greater. 'Healing' or roofing with stone was a skilled craft, and a Horsham 'sclatter' was employed on the roof of the hall for the Drapers' Guild in London in 1425. Even in the churchwardens' accounts for the early 17th-century, 'healers' earned twice or three times as much as other craftsmen.

This type of roof construction, based on crown-posts and a collar-purlin, used a great deal of timber, and was fine while wood was still plentiful, and while daily life was based around the open hall, with not much more than cramped sleeping lofts at the floored ends of houses. Cross-wings — boxes set at right angles — could give more head height at first-floor level, but still wasted much roof space. The next development in roof construction used less timber and opened up more usable roof space.

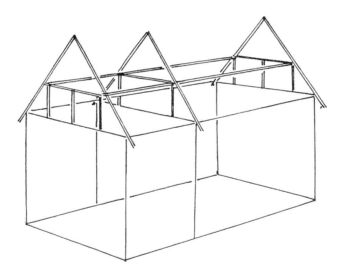

Instead of a central purlin resting on crown-posts and carrying collared rafters, two purlins were run along the sides of the roof, supported at each tie by a strut arrangement, known as *queen struts*. There were usually two vertical struts at each tie, or bay division, although a third central one was often added on the end wall, and sometimes they were set at an angle, but the principal was the same.

It is fairly safe to say that no houses were built with crown-post roofs after about 1520, although there was almost certainly an overlap period, so identifying the roof construction is one of the most important points when trying to put a date on the original erection of a timber-framed house. The insertion of chimneys and upper floors sometimes led to quite extraordinary feats of adaptation, which make even this basic task a problem! Although we often complain about the mutilation of fine roofs by subsequent up-dating, we cannot really blame our ancestors for whole-heartedly adopting the built-in chimney, which meant that no longer did they have to live *inside* what amounted to a large chimney — the open hall house.

It is clear that, for most people living in and around Horsham before 1500, the term 'builder' would be almost synonymous with 'carpenter'. Workers in stone — masons, stone layers and healers — played some part at the beginning and end of house-building, under-pinning sills, laying floors and putting on the roof, but the lion's share of the work still belonged to the sawyers, carpenters and joiners. Although there is evidence for Roman kilns in the area, towards Ifield and Rudgwick, the first documentary reference I have found of anything similar for the vicinity of Horsham is to the death of Henry Soche, 'bryckmaker', in 1555, and in 1623, John Stephens, 'bricklayer', appears in the churchwardens' accounts.

From early records and illustrations we know that some of the methods and many of the tools used by carpenters have altered very little. L. F. Salzman's standard work on documentary records of building — *Building in England down to 1540* — identifies several different kinds of axes, hammers and saws, adzes, planes, chisels, files, awls, pincers, and augers or gimlets, none of which would be strange to the modern carpenter. An illustration from 1531 shows compasses, set-square, box-plane, chisel, augers, axes and saws, and, while two carpenters measure with a line, the third steadies the wood he is working across carpenters' trestles (*see* illustration 8).

5. The principal posts, eave-plate and some intermediate timbering of the side-wall of a three-bay timber-framed building, once visible in the car-park of the *King's Head*, Horsham (1985), now demolished.

6.   The crown-posts, bracing and collar-purlin exposed during the demolition of Bornes, a burgage house which stood on the site of Boots, in the Carfax.

7.   Intermediate framing and diagonal bracing on the north side of a building on Talbots Alley. The small panels and straight diagonals suggest a date at the end of the 16th/beginning of the 17th century, or even later.

8. Carpenters constructing a timber-framed building (1531).

A note on burgage holdings in Horsham

Horsham was first mentioned as a borough in 1235, and was probably given this status
by 1210. The town was a 'burgage-tenure borough', which meant that the right to vote
— both in matters of local administration and parliamentary representation — originally
went, as we have seen, to the most important local residents who were owner-occupiers.
However, as time went by, the vote became attached to the plot, rather than to the
burgage holder or even his house.

This system was much abused later, when votes remained attached to plots that had
become divided into small portions, or where there was no longer a house, and the
right to vote could be used by whoever owned the freehold of the estate, whether he
lived in the town or not.

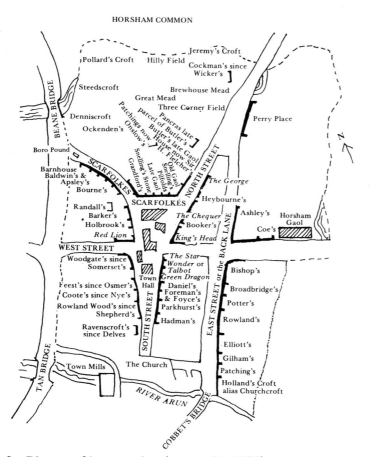

9. Diagram of burgage plots (as traced in 1792).

The 52 original bur-
gages, at one shilling a
year rent, seem to have
remained intact until
1439, but by 1502 there
were 57 for 52s. 6d., and
in the first known written
survey, of 1611, there
were 54 at 52 shillings.
The diagram that is usu-
ally presented with this
survey was not drawn up
until 1792, and copied
again for William Albery's
books in about 1927, so
is only a guide. From
studying the written rec-
ords and comparing these
with the few maps of the
town that exist, especially
the 1844 tithe map, it is
clear that the burgage
holdings were originally
rectangular, most running
back from the market
area to the north/south
ways to the east and
west. Those burgages
that became divided
most and earliest, ran along each side of the tracks that became East Street and West
Street.

As the early owners/occupiers of burgage holdings were likely to have been the wealthiest and most influential residents, these are the most promising sites to investigate for early houses. As they were also gathered around the heart of the town — Skarfolkes, Carfax, the market-place — they also present some of the best examples of continuing development and adaptation.

Plan and elevation of 13/15 East Street, a recent discovery.

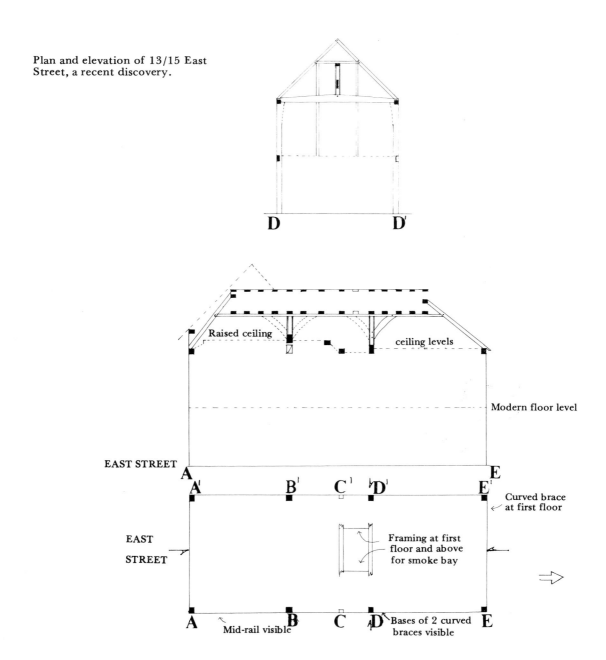

PART TWO

THE BUILDINGS

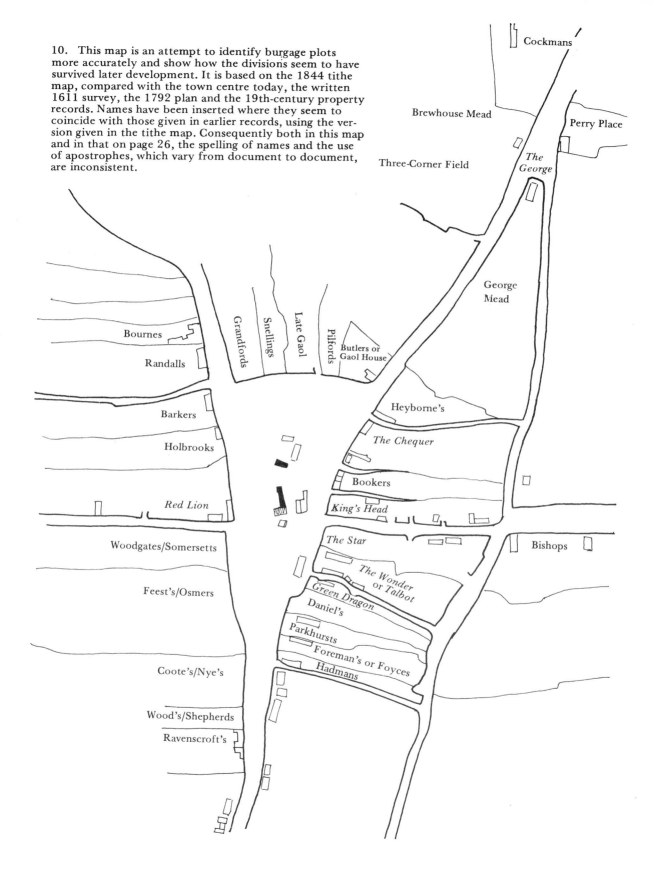

10. This map is an attempt to identify burgage plots more accurately and show how the divisions seem to have survived later development. It is based on the 1844 tithe map, compared with the town centre today, the written 1611 survey, the 1792 plan and the 19th-century property records. Names have been inserted where they seem to coincide with those given in earlier records, using the version given in the tithe map. Consequently both in this map and in that on page 26, the spelling of names and the use of apostrophes, which vary from document to document, are inconsistent.

Cockmans

Brewhouse Mead

Perry Place

Three-Corner Field

The George

George Mead

Bournes

Randalls

Grandfords

Snellings

Late Gaol

Pilfords

Butlers or Gaol House

Heyborne's

Barkers

The Chequer

Holbrooks

Bookers

Red Lion

King's Head

Woodgates/Somersetts

The Star

Bishops

The Wonder or Talbot

Feest's/Osmers

Green Dragon

Daniel's

Parkhursts

Foreman's or Foyces

Hadmans

Coote's/Nye's

Wood's/Shepherds

Ravenscroft's

PERRY PLACE

Although this is called a burgage by 1809, it does not feature in the 1611 survey, and may have been the result of splitting, either of the Cockmans burgage (now Park House site), or *The George* or Bottings (opposite Sun Alliance). The house was certainly medieval, a hall-house with two cross-wings, probably jettied at the front. The crown-posts are visible on the gables of the cross-wings, and the later chimney is in the usual place for such an insertion, in the middle of the hall range. In 1912-13 the house was demolished, and the materials used for Fullers, at Mannings Heath, which was constructed on the same plan.

This kind of house was a type that was considered rare in the Weald. As late as 1969 R. T. Mason, author of *Framed Buildings of the Weald*, wrote that 'the occupant of a cross-winged house was clearly a man of some local importance'. A number of this type of early house have now been identified in Horsham.

The subsidy list for 1524–5 lists several residents who might have qualified to live in such a house: Margery Wodsyll and John Bedyll, with his servant William Prest, were taxed at over £20, Emery Tusman and John Alynson over six pounds. Documents in the Arundel collection on the property only date back to 1662, although such a house clearly dates from the period before 1520. In 1809, the attached land was also called White's Field, and it was identified as having been at one time part of Matthew White's estate. The White family were of some local importance in the 17th century when they appear regularly as churchwardens, surveyors of highways, and so on. The early male members of the family were probably blacksmiths, although by the late 17th century they were variously described as 'gent', and one Matthew White became a citizen and merchant tailor in London before he died in the 1660s. Several male Whites were overseers of the Free School — Collyer's — and a Richard White was killed by a blow from a stick wielded by his neighbour, John Brown, in 1641.

The burgage rental was only 6d., suggesting that it was a portion, and by 1791 it was conveyed as four separate dwellings.

11.   Perry Place, *c*. 1900. A hall-house with two cross-wings. (Moved to Mannings Heath *c*. 1912.)

12.   Fullers, Goldings Lane, Mannings Heath. This was constructed about 1912 with materials from Perry Place, to a similar plan.

BOTTINGS OR *THE GEORGE*

From outside this building is clearly a hall-house with two cross-wings, that has had a floor and chimney inserted into the originally open hall. Drawings show that the southern cross-wing is of a later style, later 16th or early 17th century, but given the building's size and importance as a burgage, and the evidence from other houses, it is very probable that this cross-wing replaced an earlier one, that may have been destroyed by fire. The crown-post in the northern cross-wing has quite an individual shape, also found in a building in the Carfax, suggesting the same carpenter. Until the 1970s, there was a distinctive Tudor porch on the side of the southern cross-wing.

Title deeds on the house go back to 1555, and there is a John Botting on the subsidy list of 1524–5, living in North Street. Two Johns appear in the parish registers in the mid-16th century, probably father and son, and both butchers, and there was another branch of the family at Warnham. By 1588, it belonged to Henry Botting, who had six children, and whose only son, Harry, had had eight children, including four surviving sons, by 1634.

By the 1611 survey, it appears as 'the George, late Bottings', included four acres, was two and a half burgages, and belonged to William Slater, the elder. The George Mead, also called Jenden's, was later separated off from *The George*, and consisted of the triangular site down as far as Copnall Way. In the 18th century various tenants included Ralph Joanes, mason, and Richard Cock, tallow chandler, and by 1816, it had come into the hands of Mrs. Edward Dubbins, from her deceased husband, a surgeon. Both *The George* and Perry Place had been part of the estate of John Wicker of Park House, at one time.

13. *The George*, formerly Bottings, after renovations in the 1970s. The northern wing was renovated in 1984.

14.   The Tudor porch, which disappeared during the renovations.

15.   A crown-post in the northern wing. Note the distinctive shape of the top of the crown-post where it is pegged to the collar-purlin.

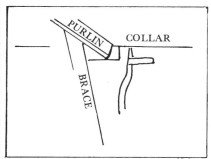

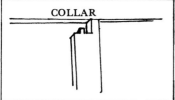

COLLAR

16. The sooted crown-post that once stood over the open hall. It has the tenon remaining from the same distinctive assembly as shown in the previous diagram, although the purlin is missing.

17. Plan and elevation of Bottings.

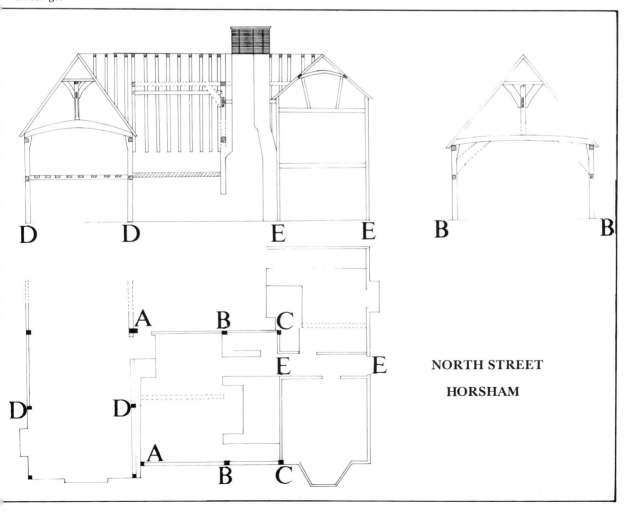

D   D   E   E   B   B

A   B   C

E   E

D   D

A

B   C

NORTH STREET

HORSHAM

BUTLERS, SOMETIME THE GAOL HOUSE

Since the Assizes were held in Horsham by 1306, alternating with Lewes, Chichester and Guildford, there is a very strong case for the existence of some kind of lock-up for prisoners, and a market town would almost certainly have needed such a facility, even if it had only been a single cell in the market hall. From 1541, the parish register for Horsham contains references to the burial of prisoners from the gaol, which was traditionally associated with the northern side of the Carfax, which was often referred to as 'Gaol Green'. In 1578, a man was hanged at Southwark for murdering the Horsham gaoler in a field there, so it follows there was a Horsham gaol, and only six years later Richard Lentot or Lintott, cooper, of Horsham, willed the 'greate howse sometime the Gaile howse with a garden on the west side' to his brother Nicholas, who also inherited Smallwells croft, the Great Field and three-cornered croft. His brother William inherited a house adjacent called Butlers, and two crofts of seven acres. A property called 'Snellings sometimes Smallwells' near Gaol Green features in the Arundel records of 1816, by then much built-upon, and from these and older pieces of evidence it is fairly safe to assume that the Gaol House and Butlers occupied the north-eastern corner of Carfax, where North Street leads out.

From a will of 1520, we know that John Rede married Elizabeth Smallwell, who died in 1522, and the 1524–5 subsidies record both a Henry Snelling and a John. Henry Snelling's will in 1552 left ten sheep to be farmed for the benefit of the local poor. As for the name 'Butler', Galfrid le Boteler appears as one of the wealthier burgesses in 1296, and we find John Butiler in 1327 and 1332. In 1447 a second chantry was founded in the parish church in memory of Henry Boteler and his wife, who had represented Horsham at seven parliaments. When surveys were made of chantry endowments before they were dissolved in the 1540s, Butlers was worth £8 6s. 5½d. a year, which included property mentioned in North Street and Skarfolks.

Only three years after Nicholas Lintott inherited from his brother, he made a covenant with the High Sheriff of Sussex, Thomas Pelham, whereby he acted as gaol keeper, and undertook to receive and deliver prisoners in return for fines and fees — in other words, he 'farmed' the Gaol! By 1611, John Lintott, son and heir of Richard (of Southwater) held 'a certain house called the Gaol House' and the adjoining messuage 'called Butlers, sometime the Gaol House' which properties amounted to 5½ burgages. In 1640, the gaol was moved along the north side of the Carfax, a move reflected in documents of 1659, when John Lintott conveyed the 'gaol or gaol house . . . near unto or opposite the George Inn or tavern . . . and all and every that ancient pile of stone buildings formerly used for a common gaol or ward for prisoners' to Richard Luckins. There are documents dating from this exchange in the Arundel collection, which mention two messuages 'one whereof lately rebuilt . . . commonly known as part of the Old Gaol or Gaol House in Scarfolkes with part in North Street' in 1816. In Albery's *Millenium* there is a drawing of the northern side of the Carfax, including what was called the Gaoler's House, dated around 1840, by Thomas Mann, and Albery states that this was pulled down in 1860.

When it became more widely known that I was ferreting around for early buildings, I was 'tipped off' that there were still a quantity of beams that looked interesting in the building on the corner of Carfax and North Street — the old Gaoler's House site. I ingratiated myself with several businesses which now occupy this property, all of whom were very helpful, and managed to trace out the plan of an L-shaped building, that was one-and-a-half storeys high, and had a double-jettied gable front.

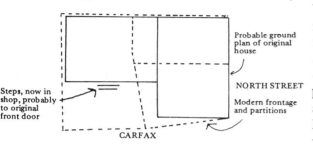

Probable ground plan of original house

NORTH STREET

Modern frontage and partitions

Steps, now in shop, probably to original front door

CARFAX

Within Vinds is the remains of a richly moulded doorway, and several of the large roof trusses, and above the Bible Bookshop and the opticians many of the moulded ceiling joists and girders are still visible. It probably looked like most people's idea of an 'Elizabethan' town-house, and may well have been the house left in Richard Lintott's will of 1584. By the time of Thomas Mann's drawing it had been largely encased in brick, and was obviously further rendered, encased and the frontage altered when the adjacent terrace was put up. Perhaps this is why Albery thought that it had been demolished. It remains to be more fully drawn and recorded.

18. Thomas Mann's drawing of the Carfax, north side, c. 1840, showing the Gaoler's House, bottom right.

19. The gable end of the Gaoler's House, still recognisable on the corner of North Street where it enters the Carfax.

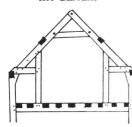

(*left*) Roof constructed with 'interrupted' or 'dropped tie'.

20. One of the 'interrupted' or 'dropped' ties, a device which gained extra room in the attic storey.

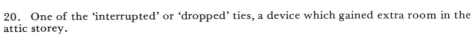

21. A girder and joists in a first-floor chamber looking onto North Street. The edges of the timbers are finely chamfered and 'stopped'.

22. Looking out of Skarfolkes (Carfax) up North Street, about 1620. The reconstructed appearances of the buildings are based on what remains today of the Gaoler's House, *The King of Prussia*, and two buildings on the Chequer burgage.

23.   Carfax Club, Horsham, 1912.

24.   The same view in 1984. The only remaining medieval building on this burgage site (Heyborne's, late Bookers in 1611) is a five-bay hall-house whose end gable is concealed behind the 'John Gorman' front. The Central Market building was probably the 17th/18th-century inn called *The King of Prussia*, which probably included the earlier range.

Bournes/Bornes; Heybournes/Heybornes: spelling was not standardised until well into the 19th century, so names of people and properties in written records are often spelt in different ways even within the same document.

28. A rather mutilated part of the medieval roof, showing sooted rafters (right) and an inserted prop lying above the collars which tie each pair of rafters.

29. Plan and elevation of Bookers, Nye's or *The King of Prussia* also Heyborne's.

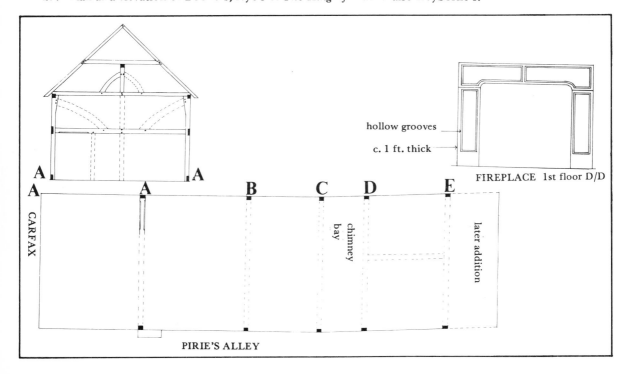

30. A wealden at Battle, *The Pilgrim's Rest*, with jettied ends showing framing from two periods of building.

31. The crown-post that stood over the open hall of the wealden on the Chequer site in Horsham.

THE CHEQUER

This site, rented as one and a half burgages in 1611, was then owned by Thomas Smythe through his wife Elizabeth, born a Jenner, who had inherited from her brother, John. She died in 1620, but her husband outlived her by 11 years. The northernmost boundary of the site seems to have been Pirie's Alley, and it may well have stretched as far as the south side of the *Stout House*, or even a block farther, where the alley runs down to the auction rooms. Two of the present buildings were there in 1611 — the long range that has at various times contained Oldershaw's, Acres, Lovetts, and now has Bridgers and Rosie's (26/28), and a concealed portion of what is at present The Frame Shop. This was more apparent in early postcards and photographs that appeared before the 1920s, as Durrants. Parts of the *Stout House* may also have existed in 1611.

The characteristic hall house of Kent and Sussex is a type that has come to be called a 'wealden' because it has been found so often in the Weald. It is built like a rectangular box, usually with a two-bay hall with a crown-post on an open tie above it, and floored bays each end, one which would have contained the parlour and solar or private chamber over, and other which contained the kitchen, buttery and service rooms generally. It was all under one roof, and because the ends were often jettied along the front, the hall appeared recessed, and often had extra support in the shape of arch braces each side to the eave plate. Some of the houses were also jettied around the side, which meant that the floor joists had to be 'herring-boned' off a diagonal beam called a 'dragon'. Wealdens were generally large, except perhaps in towns where sites were more restricted, and were indicative of wealth. At the end of the hall which backed onto the solar bay, where the owner of the house would sit at his table, the partition would often be some form of panelling below the girder or beam which tied the two principal posts at first-floor level. To one side would have been the door leading into the parlour from the hall. The wooden screen, and certainly the 'dais' beam gave scope for demonstrations of luxury, and were often moulded and carved, and finely jointed. The open tie with its crown-post could also be moulded, chamfered and decorated. It is generally accepted that houses of this type were not being built after about 1420, and some were as early as 1380, so it is likely that this is the earliest house left on the Chequer site, and is one of three wealdens that can still be seen in Horsham, each slightly different.

32. The door-head and remains of the moulded dais beam at the southern end of the hall of the Chequer wealden.

33. Carfax, east side, *c.* 1870, showing the gable front of Durrants, between the wealden and the *Stout House*.

34. Durrants, after re-structuring for the 1920s foyer of a cinema/theatre.

35. Wealden, south of Pirie's Alley. Shop divisions reflect the bay divisions of the original building. The gable window was inserted after the hall was floored over, and enlarged in the 19th century.

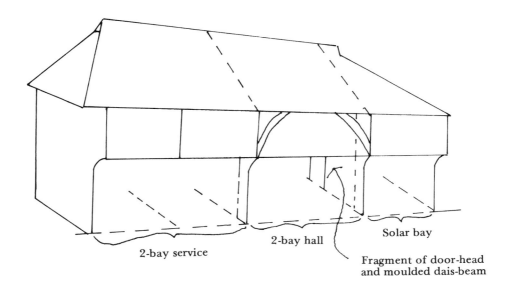

2-bay service   2-bay hall   Solar bay

Fragment of door-head
and moulded dais-beam

36.   Diagram of the wealden on the Chequer site.

An early photograph shows the gable-ended building that was once adjacent to the wealden, then occupied by Durrants, but the formation of a theatre foyer in the early 20th century seemed to have demolished this. The *Stout House* has some interesting features at the side — which seems jettied — and at the back, where the rafter ends are visible. When I first went into this building, I found timbering in a ground floor store-room which did not seem to fit the plan and shape of the pub or go with the remains of small-square panelling at the rear. This was a case where I was sure the roof would provide the answers — and it did, though not quite in the way I had expected.

The roof of the *Stout House* was quite clearly post-1550, with side-purlins, but it was constructed largely out of re-used and sooted medieval timbers, obviously from an older hall-house. Turning away from this roof I found myself looking down on an intact section of medieval roof, with the brace from a crown-post reaching up to the purlin that stopped just behind the hexagonal window above the Frame Shop. Clambering down and crawling under the tie I found myself inside what had been one bay of an upper chamber, a crown-post at each end. It became clear that this had extended another bay in each direction, because of the pattern of up-braces, and the store-room timbering was obviously the remains of the ground-floor below the third bay back from the Carfax. There was no sooting, supporting the idea that these were upper chamber bays, and bearing in mind the other houses I knew of in Horsham, it may well have been the cross-wing to a hall which was formerly on the *Stout House* site, and possibly from whose timbers the *Stout House* was constructed in an up-dating rebuild. Moreover, one of the crown-posts had the same curious shape as the crown-post in

Bottings' northern cross-wing. Perhaps we are looking at the work of the same carpenter!

In 1611, only one messuage is mentioned on the site, although as another one and a half burgage plot adjoined, present uncertainty about the plot boundaries could account for this. By 1809 there were some five houses, incorporating shops, and a barn, slaughter-house and stable. The barn off Pirie's Alley may well have been one of these ancillary buildings — such a building *was* also mentioned in 1611. In 1816 one of the messuages or tenements is described as 'containing three low rooms, two chambers (usually first floor rooms) a cellar and a new stair, lately erected', and another 'low room' was a smith's shop. Among the various tenants in the last decades of the 18th century and the beginning of the 19th, were Samuel Bryan, baker, Samuel Caffin, Richard Joanes, mason, William Weller, weaver, Robert Grace, currier and James Potter, another baker. The complex of buildings at one time had at least eight tenants, and clearly more than one of the rooms that opened onto the street were used as shops.

The owner of the burgage site in 1611, Thomas Smyth, died in 1631, and an inventory was taken of his goods. One of the items consists of those things 'in his howse called the checker dyvers ?stenderds as table frames formes chares and courtenrods . . . xxx s'. In the house in which he was living, which contained a 'canopi chamber and the newe chamber' as well as a parlour, were listed a silver bowl and six silver spoons and two green rugs, as well as two beds and all the linen and bedding to go with them. The whole inventory totalled over £59.

37. The roof timbers of the *Stout House* looking south. Note re-use of medieval sooted rafters — possibly a rebuild of the hall range to the Durrants' cross-wing.

38. The rafters and brace of the crown-post at B/B (*see* drawing) of Durrants' cross-wing.

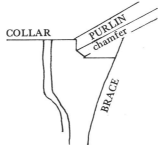

COLLAR PURLIN chamfer BRACE

39. Durrants' cross-wing: crown-post on tie at B/B.

40. Durrants' cross-wing: crown-post at A/A shows the same distinctive assembly as in Bottings on North Street.

41. Durrants' cross-wing: brace to tie A/A.
42. Plan and elevation of 28 Carfax, Horsham.

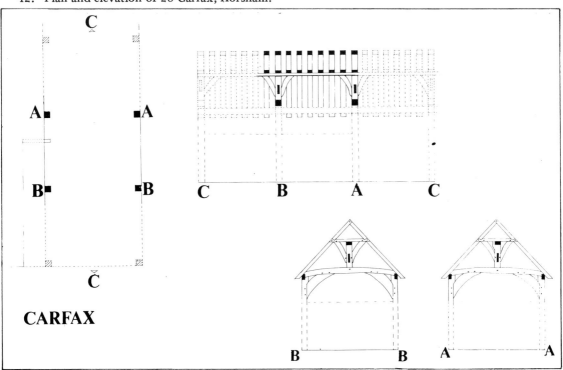

CARFAX

THE *KING'S HEAD*

The residents of Horsham, and visitors to the town, have certainly been drinking and eating in buildings on the *King's Head* site for many decades, although there is no indication that it was an inn on the 1611 survey, when the whole corner site, which probably included the buildings now occupied by several shops, was one and a half burgages, belonging to James and Dionisia Veraye. Dionisia (or Denise) had been a Jenner, sister to Elizabeth Smythe (who had inherited the Chequer, next door) and *her* inheritance from her brother, John, was this property, which then contained two houses, two shops and a horsemill. The present range of small shops and offices, adjacent to the *King's Head* on the east side of Carfax are timber-framed, and evidence of previous jettying is still visible over the present antique shop. One wall of another building that must have been part of this complex remains in the car-park behind, and more work needs to be done on interpreting and unravelling these buildings. From visual evidence, the oldest part of the *King's Head* seems to be the range containing the main entrance, which just shows the remains of a hip.

Records alone show how much this building has been altered and added to in the last 300 years: by 1809, there were a brewhouse, stables, a coachhouse, and other offices with the 'messuage or inn', and in 1777 we read that the owner, Lady Irwin, had purchased the adjoining property with a view to improving the inn . . . indeed, by 1816 she had achieved this by demolishing a cottage next door to 'render the avenues to the *King's Head* more commodious'! By that year, the site is described as being bounded by North and East Streets, and having a millhouse, granaries, store house and shops, in addition to the previously mentioned buildings. Various tenants had come and gone – Arthur Rowland, 'gent', who appears as a burgess in the second half of the 17th century, the Cooks, husband and widow, and at that time (1816) Thomas Lee. It would be interesting to discover the source of the date above the main entrance, which is more likely to refer to burgage history than the present buildings, although these still have to be fully recorded.

43. Buildings adjacent to the *King's Head*. Note brackets on centre shop indicating earlier jetty, and change in roof levels showing two separate builds.

44. The *King's Head,*
c. 1890.

45. The *King's Head,*
c. 1912.

46. The *King's Head,*
1984.

THE *WONDER* OR TALBOT

There is good reason to suppose that East Street was originally the way between two burgage sites, which, because it led out in direct line towards St Leonards, became a thoroughfare. The houses along the north and south sides were built, from early times, on parts of the burgage plots which ran back as far as the line of Park Street–Denne Road. In 1611, the area which corresponds most closely to the corner of East Street, where it enters Market Square, was listed as two portions of burgages, one belonging to Thomas and Mary Sheppard at fourpence, the other to John Wood at threepence. Each is described as having a house and barn, garden and orchard. Two medieval houses were definitely here, north of Talbot or Pump Alley – now (1985) The River Kwai Restaurant and a private cottage, and 3–4 bays that ran back from what is now the Trustee Savings Bank, and were known as the Stuart Cafe in 1968, when it was demolished. All that remains of this are some drawings, which suggest that it was similar to the ranges that existed on the Heyborne's site, and next to the *Stout House.*

The house that runs along the north side of the alley, butting up to ancillary buildings with queen struts and the small square panelling that indicates post-medieval build, seems to be a complete hall-house of five bays, with a two-bay hall. The crown-post that stood above the open hall has been mutilated when the late-16th-century chimney was inserted and the hall floored over. A heavily-sooted partition crown-post exists still at the eastern end, and when the occupants of the cottage at that end were doing some repairs (in 1983) they came across the remains of the spandrel and tie that went up to one side of the open truss, showing beautifully how a medieval carpenter assembled four of the main components of a house. Much of the exterior timbering has been replaced, but the ends of the heavy medieval rafters and much of the eave-plate are still clearly visible, as is one early curved brace. Some of the original large panelling can be seen on the north side of the building from a rear car-park.

On the south side of Talbot–Pump Alley is another remnant of a medieval range, of two to three bays, at the rear of Hoad & Taylor. Another one to two bays were probably demolished when the post-medieval building was erected on the Market Square end, still in the timber-frame tradition, but with side purlins and higher ceilings, matching a similar addition north of the alley. The side framing of both these additions can be seen in the walls of the archway leading into the alley. When the medieval range of Hoad & Taylor's was examined, it was clear that the roof had been lowered, as the stock of the crown-post was reduced and the collar purlin badly mutilated. The principal posts are quite massive for such a narrow building, which could have been the cross-wing for a hall, now gone, that may have run to the south. The wedge-shaped notches for keeping the props in place when the frame was hauled into place are still visible on the alley side of two principal posts.

47. *(above)* North of Talbot Lane on part of the burgage called variously the *Star*, or *Wonder*, or *Talbot*. A fairly complete hall-house of five bays.

48. *(right)* A sketch of the probable bay divisions of the house in illustration 47, the crown-post over the open-hall would have been at B and has been cut away by the inserted chimney. Much of the timbering has been replaced, but a characteristic curved-brace remains.

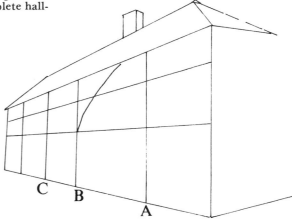

49. *(left)* The partition crown-post at C looking from the west.

50. *(left)* The soot-encrusted partition crown-post that stands on the tie at A with original wattle-and-daub infill.

51. *(below)* One end of the tie at B showing the jointing of the tie to principal post, eave plate and rafter, and how the three-cornered brace or spandrel was pegged into the chamfered principal. (See also sketch)

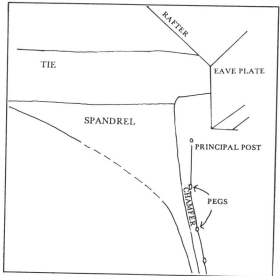

60. *(right)* Causeway House (Horsham Museum). Enough of the crown-posted medieval core of this house can be traced to establish the outline of a four-bay hall house around which was constructed a most impressive late 16th/early 17th century framed-house, double-jettied at the front with oriel windows, which were replaced by bay windows in the 18th century.

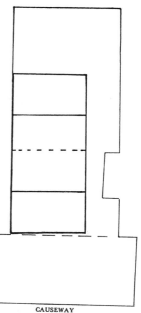

CAUSEWAY

61. *(above)* A reconstruction of the probable appearance of the 'Tudor' front before it was plastered over in the 18th century.

62. *(right)* The four-bay timber-framed building which constitutes the core of the present building.

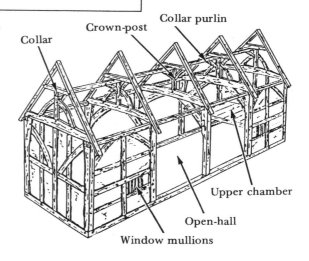

Collar

Crown-post

Collar purlin

Upper chamber

Open-hall

Window mullions

PARKHURSTS, AND HADMAN'S

Beyond the Museum building it is difficult to disentangle the burgage holdings from a mass of later additions, extensions and re-allocation. Morin Gardens does seem to mark the end of the borough holdings and the beginning of church property, although the alley may have had its line altered slightly once or twice, so it seems that Causeway Lodge is probably on the site of the part-burgage, 'one messuage with a Backside and garden adjoining' belonging to Edward and Elizabeth Parkhurst in 1611, although it may also be on the part-burgage of 'late Foreman's and formerly Foyces'. The present house is timber-framed within its rendered shell, but the side-purlin roof and the style of the framing suggest a date for building of somewhere at the end of the 16th century, or the beginning of the 17th.

The name of 'Foyce' — now Voice, and earlier Foys — is one that crops up often in the early history of the town. Elizabeth Foys was taxed as living in South Street in 1524, a wealthy widow, and her son, Harry, seemed to have been living with her. There is a small brass now let into a pillar in the parish church, which is recorded as being of Elizabeth Foys. It was once on a gravestone at the west end of the central aisle, with one to her husband Richard. As the inscription read 'Here lieth Richard Foys and Elizabeth his wife, which Richard deceased the 22nd day of April, the yere 1513: o thir souls Ihu have m'cy', and Richard's will left a house and lands called Cobetts, Gylhams and Holondes to his widow, she must have followed the custom of the time, having her brass ordered and made at the same time as her husband's to be mounted when she died. Her eldest son, George, died in 1521, leaving 20s. 0d. towards a 'sute' of white vestments for high feasts, and £60 for his daughter Elizabeth, when she reached seventeen. She was first cousin to that other Elizabeth, who first married Richard Bishop, and then bore a bastard to Thomas Bradbridge. Harry or Henry Foys, George's younger brother, did not die until 1550. Foremans was almost certainly a reference to the family that produced two parish clerks and a master at Collyers in the 17th century. Causeway House may well have replaced one or two earlier properties.

Numbers 11 and 12 Causeway, very probably Hadman's, may well have been one house originally — a hall-house with a cross-wing, jettied at the front. Although I have not yet been able to study these houses in detail, from brief descriptions, observation, and my knowledge of other Horsham buildings, it would seem quite likely that there was a two-bay hall with a floored service bay to the north, and a floored cross-wing to the south. In 1611, Henry Patching held Hadman's, and when he died, in 1614, his inventory listed 12 rooms, including a shop, in which there were six shelves and 'one shoopborde'. Although he was a tailor, unfortunately his stock was not listed, but among some of the items in his house, were 'two painted beedseelings' — probably decorated hangings for a four-poster — in the room above the shop, a great chest in the room above the parlour, and 14 pieces of pewter, two chamber pots and a bible, kept in the kitchen!

63. Causeway Lodge, no. 10, a post-medieval timber-framed building with later rendering.

64. Nos. 11 & 12 Causeway, probably Hadman's, a hall house with a cross-wing, occupied by Henry Patching, tailor, at the time of his death in 1614.

RAVENSCROFT'S, LATE NUTLEY'S

From old photographs of this property (now called Minstrels, 29–30 Causeway), it is easier to see that it is two separate houses, as the southern range then had a Victorian brick façade, the northern range being weather-boarded. At that time the northern range was divided again into two cottages, the northernmost having the shop front of 'Randall, breeches maker' and the southern being occupied by Vaughan, at one time a bootmaker and cobbler. The 19th-century Post Office directories show that a number of Causeway houses were commercial premises of one sort or another, at a time when tradespeople still lived 'on the job'.

More significant for the earlier history of these two houses are other points that came to light when the Calburns commenced buying and renovating in the 1930s. Robert Calburn kept an invaluable account of the proceedings, during the course of which an 1887 solicitors' report revealed the existence of a rent book on the property dating from 1677, by which time, at least, it appeared to be glebe land – that is, vicarage property, and had housed both parish clerk and sexton. Whether this had always been the parish clerk's house, rather than Flagstones, or whether it had become so after that house ceased to be church property, is not altogether clear. In the 1524 subsidy under South Street (which then included Causeway) the parish guild or fraternity of St John the Baptist was taxed on lands rated at £8, probably part of the original endowments made in 1457. These lands could have been absorbed by the vicarage after the dissolution of the chantries about 1548, as the parish certainly assumed responsibility for the almshouses in the Normandy which were the principal concern of the fraternity. According to property deeds held at Barbican House, Lewes, on nearby houses, Minstrels seems to have formed part of the holdings of Hall Ravenscroft in 1628, and his father, John, did own a one-and-a-half burgage plot in 1611, that had previously been called Nutleys. A Richard Nutley died in 1521, and John Nutley was taxed on lands in the 1559 subsidy, although he was not in South Street in 1524.

The southern range would always have been floored in, and jettied along the front, possibly with a detached kitchen at the rear. A mullioned rear window is still visible on what has now become an internal wall. There is some evidence to suggest that the cross-wings of the northern range may have extended back another bay, making them three-bay, and the open hall would have been floored in the early 16th century. A quite impressive stone chimney-piece was discovered by the Calburns in the upper chamber of the floored hall, and moved to the room below. It resembles the four-centred hearths in Bolters, almost opposite, and it is very tempting to make connections, especially as both houses appear to have been Ravenscroft holdings.

The 'continuous jetty' style of house – the southern range – tended to be built as workshop-cum-shop-cum-living accommodation, like the range that was demolished in the Bishopric in the 1970s, and as such would almost certainly have been let to tenants. The northern range matches more closely the style of other burgage properties in the town, suggesting a certain status and standard of living, albeit originally suited to about the middle of the 15th century.

65. Minstrels, Causeway, now one house, was originally two. The northern part is a characteristic Horsham hall house with two cross-wings, each jettied at the front. The southern range was
a continuous jetty house similar to some that used to be on the northern side of the Bishopric.

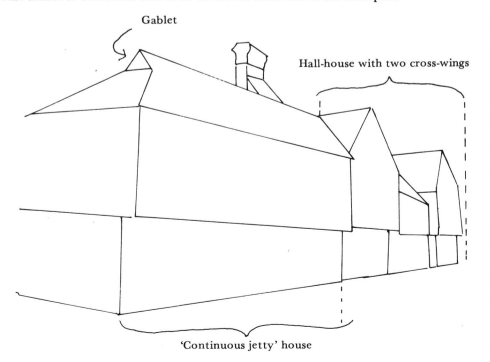

66. The carved and moulded crown-post standing on the tie that was originally over the open hall.

67. The northern side-wall of Minstrels' northern cross-wing, as revealed by work at no. 32, which now shares this wall. When no. 32 was butted up in the late 17th/early 18th century, a second eave-plate was inserted; both this and the original have dropped to the rear.

68. The crown-post over the upper chamber in the northern cross-wing, much plainer and less impressive than that over the hall.

BISHOPS, 'LATE SEALE'S', AND 'LATE ANDREW ROBINSON'S'

Comparing the 'East Street' in the 1611 survey with the 'East Street' we know today, it seems that the two were not the same street: in 1611, the name apparently referred to what we now call Park Street and Denne Road, which strengthens the theory that the present East Street was a 'twitten' between road and market-place, grown large. By the 18th century, it seems that 'East Street' did refer to the modern one, but the term was also used on some of the deeds to plots that had been on the older line, just adding to the problems that arise when trying to identify early sites and relate them to present houses.

Five houses built on burgage sites are listed in 1611 — Ashleys, which was traditionally shown as having been near the corner containing Bryce's store, Constable's or Coe's which was near the site of Brewers, Bishops late Seale's, on the corner of Denne Road and East Street, and another Parkhurst property, late Andrew Robinson's, which was down Denne Road. Of these, only two that are reasonably identifiable still exist — Bishops 'late Seale's', now the Tudor Cafe and a newsagent, and the Parkhurst house, now Arun Lodge, next to the bus depot.

Of these two, Bishops is almost certainly the earlier — a hall house of quite imposing dimensions with two cross-wings jettied at the front. Only the southern cross-wing still shows the close-studding that was visible on most of the elevations up to the mid-19th century, and which is characteristic of houses built towards the second half of the 15th century, but the carved gable boards, probably put on at the beginning of the 17th century, are still on both gables. When a floor was inserted into the hall with the addition of an internal chimney, a 'vyse' or porch was built at the back to contain the stair leading to the new upper floor. This still remains, and still contains the staircase, and recent repairs revealed the framework of a small window which once lighted the vyse.

This cross-roads was once called Stanestreet Cross, and it is tempting to suppose that this is where the burgesses, Ralph atte Stanstrete (1296 and 1327 subsidies) and Richard, probably his son (1332 subsidy), had an earlier house. Both Ralph and Richard were parliamentary representatives and Ralph was a signatory to the Holy Trinity chantry licence and owned land outside the town. The Bishops, too, were a prominent Horsham family, but not until the 16th century, when Richard Bishop, living in the Skarfolkes, was one of the wealthiest to be taxed in 1524. By the 18th and 19th centuries, the house was often known as Grace's.

69. Bishops (1984).

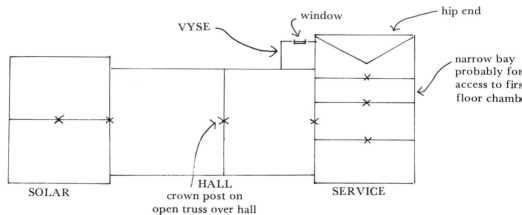

VYSE

window

hip end

narrow bay
probably for
access to firs
floor chamb

SOLAR

HALL
crown post on
open truss over hall

SERVICE

70. Bishops (19th century)
showing framing on north-
ern wing and clear jetties
to the cross-wings.

Andrew Robinson was taxed as living in East Street in 1524 at a rate that would have made him of comfortable means, but not wealthy, and probably not the owner of a house such as remains within Arun Lodge. Perhaps he lived in a humbler dwelling, and owned the land near the river, which he then sold to a family like the Parkhursts, who were certainly wealthy enough to have put up the L-shaped, Elizabethan style house that is now encased in brick and which was added to subsequently. This would have been one of the houses that went up in and around the town in the last rash of building in the truly timber-frame tradition, yet incorporating all modern conveniences like a chimney, full-height rooms at first-floor level, and even storage or servants' quarters in the loft.

71. Arun Lodge: the range at right-angles to the road (left) still contains much of the original framing, and has attic storage.

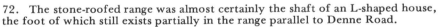

72. The stone-roofed range was almost certainly the shaft of an L-shaped house, the foot of which still exists partially in the range parallel to Denne Road.

'LOST' BURGAGES

Sometimes the only knowledge we have of medieval houses are from old photographs and documentary records. This is true of several of the burgage properties, because the same factors that have ensured that many have remained, albeit in fragments, have conversely meant that many more have gone in the successive developments and 'up-dating' of the most important part of the town — its commercial centre. Sadly, and most recently this meant the destruction of Bornes, featured in conjunction with Flagstones, which it resembled. It applies also to sites that altered much earlier.

In 1611, on the corner of West Street and Carfax, now occupied by Chart & Lawrence (1984) stood an imposing house with barns and stables, then owned by Robert Tredcroft, previously by an Agate, and earlier still by Frenches. Although Robert is described as a 'yeoman' on the inventory taken of his goods in the same year (*see* below), he was almost certainly a prosperous innkeeper by trade, as he owned not only the *Red Lion*, which gave its name to the West Street site, but also 'the house called the Anker' probably on the site in Market Square, now Lloyd's Bank.

Some 17 rooms are listed in the *Red Lion*, as well as two cellars and five other rooms that may have been in out-buildings. Several of the rooms were hung with 'paynted clothes' and had curtains and carpets. Robert himself left four jerkins, three pairs of breeches, two cloaks, one gown, four shirts and five bands to go with them, two hats and five pairs of stockings, and there were two bibles and two books of common prayer in his room, as well as quite a quantity of silver. There were 26 bedsteads scattered throughout the various rooms, some with curtains, some just 'truckles', so the degree of comfort visitors enjoyed probably depended on the price they paid! The goods and fittings in the two properties totalled over £200, a not inconsiderable sum when the average day wage was a shilling for a skilled carpenter.

73. 'The Red Lion, formerly Frenches, late Agates'. Two views of what was once a large burgage plot running back from Skarfolkes (Carfax) nearly as far as the Springfield Road. By 1611 it was already divided into four or five portions. (Now Chart & Lawrence, 1984).

In 1637 an inventory was taken on the goods of Richard Hurst, amounting in value to £128, and from the description it is almost certain this was the same property, not including the 'Ancker'. The 1898 photograph of 'George Duke's Emporium' is almost certainly this house, especially when taken with the picture of the aftermath of a 20th-century fire on the site, showing the timbering characteristic of a house of the mid-16th century, similar to 'Bolters' front range in the Causeway. Some vestiges may still be embedded in the corner of Chart & Lawrence.

'The true inventory . . . of howshold stuffe of Robert Tredcraft of Horsham . . . deceased . . . 1611 . . . taken and praysed by Richard White, Edward Parkhurst, Thomas May and Thomas Sharpe . . .' (WSRO EP1/29/106/2)

In the (upper) chamber

Imprimis one standinge bedstedle wth grene Curtens two lowe bedstedles ii . . . i flockbed i quilt ii Rugges iii blankettes iii coverlets iiii fetherboulsters ii fether pillowes iii payer of sheete & ii pillowes

Itm of his wearinge apparell iii . . . iiii jerkins iii payer of breeches ii clokes i gowne iiii sherts v (bands) ii hats (v) payer of stockings & ii wollen . . .
Itm one truncke wth xii payer of (pil)low cotes therein
Itm one joyned chest wth x . . . tableclothes whereof ii be diaper & xxvi towels therein
Itm one other joyned chest with ii . . . shertes therein
Itm one presse one looking glasse one litle deske & a linsey wolsey Colvercloth (?)
Itm ii bibles one old pultons abridge . . . two bookes of Comon prayer
Itm one dozen of silver spoones one alle silver salt one litle salt viii silver bowles and one beaker all wayinge allmost vi poundes
Itm one chest wth his evidencies (?) there . . . sed stoole iii litle chestes one peece of newe wollen cloth and one peece of new cawse cloth for napkins
Itm one sacke with £viii of lambes woll therein
Itm two tapestrie coverletts
Itm iii brushes i urynall & certen glasse bottles
Itm of ready money in his purse

In the Parlor

Itm ii tables wth frames i lyvery cubberd ii frmes i chayer ii carpetts one Cubberd cloth x cushions i payer of brandyrons and certen paynted cloths

In the hall

Itm ii tables i forme viii joyned stools iii chayers i cubberd one litle round table vii cushions i old carpett ii cubberd clothes i payer of brandirons i fyer panne i payer of tonges iii pot-hangers one peece of iron & certen paynted clothes

In the litle Parlor

Item ii tables i stool i cushion & one payer of playinge tables

In the chamber over the parlor

Itm ii standing bedstedles ii truckebedstedles ii fether beddes iii fether bolsters iiii pillowes ii flockbeddes iii flockboulsters iiii blanketts iiii coverings & i payer of curtens
Itm one table wth a frame i carpett i joyned forme i other forme iiii joyned stooles i chayer & i cushion

In the litle chamber at the stayers hedd

Itm one truckle bedstedle one fetherbed i blankett one boulster one pillowe one presse i chest one hamper and shelves

In the middle chamber

Itm ii bedstedles i fetherbedd i fether boulster i pillow ii flockbeddes ii boulsters (ii) coveringes & one blankett

In the Parlor chamber

Itm two bedstedles one payer of curtens ii fetherbeddes three fether boulsters one flocke boulster two coveringes two blankets & fowre pillows

Itm one table and frame five stooles one joyned forme one other forme two chayers one cushion & one carpett

In the chamber over the hall

Itm one standinge bedstedle one fetherbedd ii fetherboulsters two pillowes one Rugge ii mattres i blankett and curtens

Itm one cubbere i lyvery table i longe table wth a frame two joyned formes one liverie cubberd viii cushions ix stooles one carpett one chayer one payer of brandirons one payer of bellowes one empty chest one payer of playing tables & one white cubberd cloth

Itm one chest xi payer of sheetes therein two boxes & one litle chest wth five dozen of Fine napkins and one od one five dozen & three odd napkins of flaxe & hempe wth painted clothes about the room and curtens for the windows

In old Bottinges chamber

Itm one bedstedle wth curtens one fetherbed and boulster two pillowes one blankett one covering one truckle bedstedle wth a fether bedd and boulster two pillowes one blankett and a coveringe

Itm one wicker chayer one other chayer & fower cushions one trunke wth xliii sheetes therein and on stoole

In the Folkes chamber

Itm three bedstedles one flocked and boulster one coveringe one blanket and one payer of sheetes

In the middle Garrett

Itm two bedstedles and one lynnen tester

In the further Garrett

Itm two bedstedles one bagge of hoppes divers varyers crocks pottes & bottles one side sadle one wodd sadle £xxx of hempen tyre £xii of towe six trugges £iii of wooll and other basketts and lumberment

In the buttrie chamber

Itm two bedstedles wth curtens one downe bed & boulster two downe pillowes one fether bed and boulster two pillowes two Rugges two blanketts two mattres two payer of sheets and two pillowbeeres

Itm one table wth frame fower joyned formes two chayers three stooles one liverie cubbere one carpett one cubberd cloth viii cushions one payer of playing tables one payer of brandirons one payer of tonges the paynted clothes about the chamber and curtens for three windowes

In the Bakhowse loft

Itm two bedstedles two fetherbeddes fower fether boulsters two coveringes two blanketts one close stoole one table and one forme one stole and one skreene

In the kitchinge loft

Itm one bedstedle and curtens one fether bed & boulsters two pillows one Rugge one blankett one truckle bedstedle and one flockbedd

Itm one table wth frame three formes two stooles one chayer one cushion and the paynted cloths about the Roome

In the Brewehowse loft

Itm three payer of canvas sheets

Itm two coopes a heape of Chacke (?) a trest (?) a still a brake ii payer of bootes tenne couple of Coddfish & other lumberment

In the litle loft next

Two hoggesheddes wth salt one hogshedd wth vinegar two baskets and one flaskett

In the Brewhouse

Itm one fornece and brewing vessels a stack of wood a heape of pales . . . casks two loades of coles a wollen wheele and other lumberment

In the milkhowse

Itm one kneadinge trowe one boulting hutch i tubbe i Crock of butter i powdringe tubbe i tubbe wth pease a half bushell i tubbe wth tallowe i kymnel i hanging cubberd i charne & shelves and lumberment

Itm one tubbe wth meale viii fletches of bacon and one breast of beef

In the kitchen

Item foure iron pottes twoe brasse potts iiii dripping pannes one brasse caldron vii brasse kettles one warminge panne vii brasse posnetts & iiii chafinge dishes

Item viii spittes two frying panne fower gridirons one iron morter one stone morter one bushell measure ii racks one payer of brandirons iii pothangers one iron pale ii fire pannes and one iron to put before (frying?) pannes

Item one laten ladle one skymmer one slice ii brasse sponnes one skonce iii payer of pott-hoocks one fleshhook one clever one co . . . one shredding knife one chopping knife one breddgrater one kerne & vii lb weights and one mustard ball

Item xii woodden dishes iiii woodden platters iii potliddes iiii ladles vi dozen of trenchers iiii bucketts one cubberd one moulding table ii dressers one forme iiii shelves and one chayer

Item of pewter two square plates vi round plates iii basons iii ewers iii chargers iii dozen of pewter dishes . . . small basons iii culloners xvii platters xxvi small plates iiii dozen of s(aw)sers viii round pottengers ix square pottengers iiii candlesticks vii salce . . . shes xii chamber potts iii round cupps one egg plate xxii spoones all waying xxxiii nayle and iiii lb at viii s

In the Buttery

Itm of pewter xiii platters x . . . dishes vi basons one . . . dish . . . chamber potts two wyne . . . pottes xxi quart potts xvii pynt pote iii half pint pottes ii quarter pynt pottes two (kettles) and two saltes all waying xxiiii nayle at viii s the pounde

Item viii laten candlesticks

Itm xii stone pottes

Itm one great cubberd one litlle cubberd one bread byn vii shelves one little old chest three dozen of playing cardes vii . . . bankerd? one flaskett and one low forme

Itm vi ve . . . glasses vi napkins ii table cloths and . . .

In the Beere Cellar

Itm v Brlle whereof two full of beere

In the Wine Cellar

Itm one hogshedd of claret wyne half a hogshedd of whyte wyne one hogshedd of . . .
of wyne . . . ell . . . vyneger xi . . . hoghed & vii emty comdlette?
Itm one pewter flagon and one bucking tubbe one . . . arrers and a presse

In the Gates

xl . . . of wood
Itm two pen & . . . two ch . . . o . . . es
Item iiii t . . . ch . . .
Itm two ly . . . and two calves
Itm three hogtrowes ix peeces of tymber and one ladder
Itm . . . hammes one cow three duckes and . . .

In the Stable

Itm one half peck one gallon one curry come & one mane combe
Itm inch boords and plankes over the stable

In the Ostrie

Itm two dozen bottle of hay fowre hundred of wor . . . se? momtens? and pannell boord
one tubbe and fowre bushells of otes

In the Barne

Itm the haie by estimacion iiii lodes
Itm two ladders two pronges one shovle and one wheelebarrowe

In the feilds abrode

one mare and a cole . . . nagge seised for the heriot for xxvi s vii d

In the Garner

two quarters of malt three quarters of otes fower bushells of Rye and one shovle

In the Slayinge howse

two hundred of pales

In the Barne hired of Mr Nye

eight lodes of hay by estimacion £viii . . . lode of straw by estimacion iii s . . . a lode of
raile postes

In Buckley Wood

Itm in timber hewed sawed and standing and also in wood £vi xiii iiii

In the Garder

Itm wett clothes viz two payer of hempen sheetes one payer of holland sheetes three canvas
sheetes one table cloth viii napkins and one towell

In the howse called the Ancker
In the hall

One longe table one frame three formes one . . . and one curten at the window

In the parlor

It one longe table wth a frame one frame one curten at the windowe and two curten roddes

In the kitchinge

Itm one old table wth a frame one dressing table one forme one old chayer? and three cushions?

In the B(acke?)

dresser and one old presse

In the chamber over the old Cellar

Itm two old bedstedles

In the Gower? howse

Itm two tables fower trestles two formes and fower peeces of tymber used for benches

In the newe Cellar

... fowre short ... boord ...
Itm one ...

In the Backhowse

... ch ... two bordes ... the stable

74. The timbering revealed by a fire in 1909 suggests this may have been the 17th-century property, the *Red Lion*, referred to in the inventories of 1611 and 1637.

From a study of other old photographs of the western side of the Carfax, up to and including the site of Bornes, it is possible to fill in one or two more gaps in our understanding of the early occupation of this area. The ivy-covered house shown near to the old W.E.A. hall in the early 20th-century photograph belonged to the Lintott family and was built by 1893, when Mr. Lintott, junior, was married and set up house with his bride. An earlier photograph of this site, dated 1870, shows the low, stone-roofed medieval house that the Victorian house had replaced, almost certainly the 'messuage' that was recorded as Holbrooks in 1611, belonging to one of the Eversfield family. What can be seen of the shape suggests a wealden to match the one that remains on the Chequer.

The view taken down the old London Road — now Medwin Walk, flanked by Boots and the entrance to Swan Walk — shows not only the front of Bornes, which was demolished in 1970, but another low, stone-roofed house south of Bornes, that was obviously removed when the Capitol was built, in 1923, or thereabouts. From the picture it looks much like a hall-house, with a chimney inserted into the hall, and was probably on the burgage site called Randalls, a name that originated with the Walter Randolph who was one of Horsham's first representatives at the king's parliament.

Walter Randolph and his wife Joan were claimants in a case concerning a house and three acres, from Ralph and Isabel de Stanstrete, in 1270. He went to parliament at Westminster in November of 1295, and was taxed as the wealthiest burgess in 1296. Walter was one of the signatories to the application for the Holy Trinity chantry in 1307, but by the next subsidy or taxation of 1327 it is Roger Randolf who appears much further down the scale, so perhaps the inheritance had been divided among more than one heir — we know that Walter owned lands elsewhere in the area. In 1333 a complaint was laid by the lord of the manor, John de Mowbray, against various Horsham people, including John Randolph, for breaking into the parks at Beaubush, Knepp and St Leonard's, taking wine from coastal wrecks against the right of the lord, and assaulting his servants at Horsham. Only 11 years later John was involved in a similar case of breaking into the parks of the lord of Parham, Roger Bavent, and taking deer and fish, with one of his previous companions and a Simon Lyntot, among others.

75. Chart & Lawrence, 1984.

76. West side of Carfax, 1870, showing Lintott's works and the medieval house with a Horsham stone slab roof.

77. By 1893 the medieval house had been replaced by the Lintott's family house.

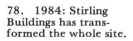

78. 1984: Stirling Buildings has transformed the whole site.

79. Looking north towards King & Chasemore's. On the left is a row of medieval houses,
including Bornes, before the Capitol was built, *c*. 1920.

80. Today King & Chasemore's is still there, but Swan Walk has swallowed up the rest.

FLAGSTONES, CAUSEWAY

Cheek by jowl with the parish church is a house which no visitor has difficulty identifying as 'old'. Now called Flagstones, it even proclaims '1615' helpfully on its gable. However, visitors are not getting the full story, for most of the building is much older than that. By tradition, Flagstones was the house of the parish clerk from the time of its construction, in the early 15th century, until the early 18th century. From the shape and framing, visible inside, it was originally a hall house with a cross-wing at the southern end. The cross-wing was jettied at the front, and in 1954, some building work revealed a tiny medieval window with wooden mullions at the gable end, now hidden once more beneath the render. The other cross-wing and extensions to the rear of the early wing came later in its history.

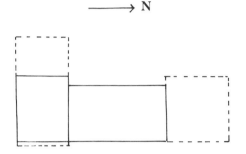

This, then, was very probably the house of the parish clerk who was left 20d. for his services by Henry Frenssh in 1423 — the first record of such an official in Horsham. Several of Horsham's early MPs were members of the Frenssh family, very likely early immigrants from the continent made good. By 1513, William Danyell was parish clerk, and held the position until he died in 1541, leaving everything to his executor, the curate Henry Patching — including the responsibility for discharging his debts! As Danyell was rated at £6 13s. 4d. in the 1524 subsidy, his position was relatively comfortable, and by the time he died, the clerk's house would probably have been 'modernised', with hearths and a chimney replacing the old open fire, and a floor inserted into the open hall, making two low rooms. Within the next 20 or 30 years the northern cross-wing would have been added, increasing the living space.

By 1610, the position carried all kinds of remunerations for duties carried out, as well as having a 'tied house'. From the Horsham churchwardens' accounts, which survive from 1610 and were written up by the then clerk, Thomas Forman, it is clear that he involved his whole family, as his wife was paid for 'washing the church cloths and skowring the pots', and his sons — he had four, and two daughters — were paid for helping him in various jobs around the church on the maintenance and repair of such items as the clock and bells. This must have helped towards the yearly rent of 6s. 8d. on a house most suited to such a large family. The eldest son, another Thomas, inherited the job after his father's death in 1626, and the youngest, Nicholas, became the assistant master or 'usher' at Collyer's Free School in 1631. In 1661, another son,

Robert, died aged 53, having been a town blacksmith, living over his business in a six-roomed house. His wife was Margery Bennet, and here may be a link to explain the next stage in the story of the house.

The inventory of Stephen Osmer, glover, who died in 1667, lists items in two ground floor rooms, and two rooms above them, and also in a 'shop chamber', implying a shop underneath, and at Thomas Bennet's house. His will makes it clear that Thomas Bennet is his son-in-law, married to his daughter Sarah, and that Stephen had been living in 'all that the south end of my dwelling howse lying next unto the Churchyard of Horsham' — surely Flagstones. Although Stephen had only been living in the south end 'conteyning two low rooms & two Chambers and one closett', three of the rooms had been tenanted by Thomas Kaine, including the kitchen, and Stephen had only occupied 'the other roome and Closett'. The will makes it very clear how the house was divided, and that the occupants of both parts should have access to a shared well, and left the whole house, the northern half being rented, to a grandchild, William.

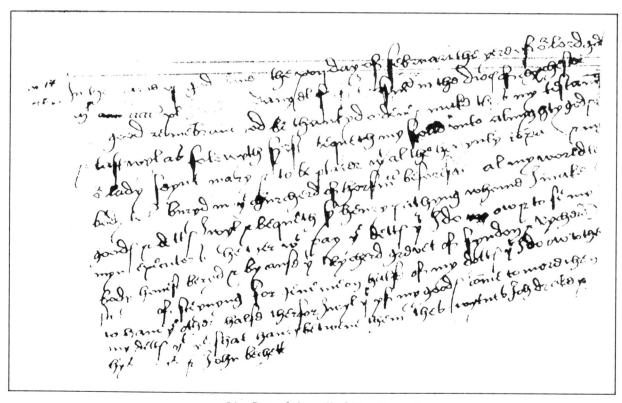

81. Part of the will of Wm. Danyell.

From this it seems that at sometime before 1667 Flagstones had ceased to be church property, and we know that there was a rent book on Minstrels (see Ravenscrofts) in 1677, as church property. It seems that the home for the clerk was moved just a few houses up the Causeway at sometime in the first half of the 17th century.

As for the date on the central gable, this probably refers to a time when the building was re-roofed, eliminating all but a few traces of crown-posting, and an enlarged gable inserted matching those on 19-20 Causeway and Bornes in the Carfax, now demolished. The carved bargeboards and pendants also matched those buildings, and there are similar barge boards on Bishops, at the top of Denne Road. Such embellishments may have been 17th-century Horsham's equivalent to double-glazing and patio doors.

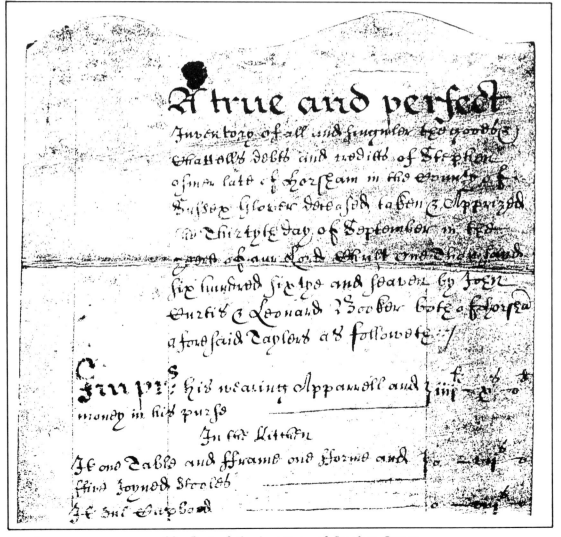

82. Part of the inventory of Stephen Osmer.

BORNES, CARFAX

As Bornes is now demolished (1970) and its site eliminated by Boots the Chemist, this is perhaps the best place to discuss it, as it was similar in several respects to Flagstones, although it never had a second cross-wing. Its original cross-wing was extended to the rear from the late 17th century onwards, as at Flagstones, and an almost identical gabled window put in for the room made by flooring the open hall. However, Bornes was not ecclesiastical, but the principal house on a burgage site, the greatest part of which belonged to Thomas Lyntott, the tailor, in 1611. The house may have taken its name from an earlier owner — John Bourne, who died in 1560, leaving 20s. to be distributed to the local poor — and was later connected in some way with the Pelhams of Laughton, as a plaque bearing their arms was built into the chimney of the extension to the cross-wing, dated 1661.

83. *(left)* Flagstones, the house mentioned in Stephen Osmer's will, 1667, but built *c.* 1400. The '1615' datestone may refer to the gable insert and decorative barge-boards.

84. *(below)* In 1954 building work was carried out on the property called Flagstones. Some of the timber-framing was revealed, and a medieval mullioned window on the left front of the southern cross-wing.

85. The cross-wing to Bornes, extended to the rear, like Flagstones. The final extension can be dated to *c.* 1661, by a plaque on a fireplace. One small medieval window survived, almost hidden under creeper. The crown-posting of this wing is shown in an earlier photograph (*see* no. 6).

86. Bornes, in London Road.

87. The original hall range with a decorated gable as at Flagstones and 19/20 Causeway, inserted when the hall was floored over. Hearths to the inserted chimney could have served rooms in both the cross-wing and the floored hall.

88. A smoke-stained crown-post photographed during demolition.

89. Bornes as it would have appeared before rebuilding.

90. Some of the Jacobean panelling in an upper room of the cross-wing.

THE FRATERNITY OF ST JOHN AND ST ANNE

In 1457, permission was given to William, Earl of Arundel, John Michelgrove, John Fust, Thomas Bradbrugge, Stephen Comber, William Gratewyke and Thomas Hoo, esquires, two clerks and eight other named parishioners of the parish church of St Mary the Virgin, Horsham, to found a gild and chantry to be based at the altar of St John the Baptist on the south side of the church. The gild was to consist of a master, four wardens, and brethren and sisters from the parishioners, who were to have the power to increase the gild, and were to hold elections for the officers annually on the Sunday after Midsummer (24 June). In the first act for the suppression of the chantries in 1545, property valued at £12 5s. 0½d. was recorded as belonging to the Brotherhood, including a 'capital messuage there called the Brothered house lying in the North street with the kitchen, stable and garden'. There is still a timber-framed house near to Horsham station, which has been known as Northchapel for decades, and this has been identified with that 'capital messuage'. It would probably not have looked quite as it does now, for several of the additions were built on after about 1550, and it may not even have been altered from the original low, open hall-house by then. When a floor was inserted into this hall, they found it necessary to raise the whole roof at the same time, and so gain usable space in the loft. They cut away the crown-posts, leaving only stumps as evidence of the original construction, and put in a side purlin roof. At the same time an outside staircase to the new upper floors was built — a vyse — which looks rather like a porch on the front. It was later extended to the west and south, in separate stages.

As late as 1622, in a deed between Nicholas Delves and John Nye with John and William Arden, mention is made of a 'messuage . . . called the Brotherhoode Hall', which had been identified with 19–20 Causeway, but which I feel may also have referred to Northchapel. The former building is now clad with white clapboard, which completely hides its unique style — it is a wealden, that is, it has a recessed hall like the Chequer, Carfax, and part of Netherledys, Blackbridge Lane, but its hall has only one bay. Both end bays were floored and jettied at the front, and the southern bay was also jettied around the side, which meant the carpenter had to use a 'dragon' beam to carry the joists around the corner.

Very close to this house is no. 18, with a complete Victorian front concealing yet another three bay hall-house. These two are similar in size and plan to the one in West Street that used to occupy the site that now contains the Gas Board showrooms.

91. Northchapel: the roof (rear)
left) with the large chimney, sits
over the old open hall-house. All
the other ranges are more characteristic of the 17th century.

92. The staircase vyse can be seen
to the left of the large gable (*see*
no. 91). The square framing immed-
iately below the eaves of the roof
was put in when the roof was
raised, as was the projecting oriel
window (left).

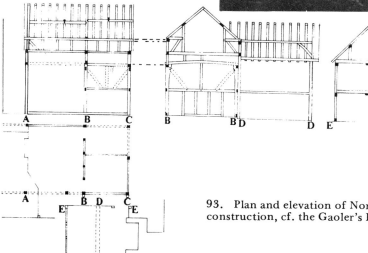

93. Plan and elevation of Northchapel showing new dropped-tie
construction, cf. the Gaoler's House.

94. *(left)* 19/20 Causeway *c*. 1895: close-studding and recessed hall still apparent, also jetty girder.

95. *(above)* 19/20 Causeway in 1984: with filled-in hall and jetties, covered with weather-board. Note the inserted gable with pendant like Bornes and Flagstones.

96. *(below)* Drawing of a wealden with a single-bay hall, as originally built.

97. The dragon-beam to bear the joists for a jetty around a corner.

98. The original doorway into the open hall with its early doorhead. Note the rebate on the girder, top left, where it was supported for the overhanging jetty.

99. One of the crown-posts to the single-bay open hall.

They all suggest that there was pressure on land for building — either because of intense development or vagaries of ownership — at a time when the norm was still for a house with an open hall, even if it had to be restricted to one bay, perhaps between about 1390 to 1430 or 1440.

100. Causeway, no. 18: another three-bay open hall-house. Framing can be seen on the side walls between this and 19/20. Notice how the edges of the roof have been lifted, 'pagoda' like, to accomodate the width of the brick front. This was once very like a house in West Street, that was on the site of the present gas showrooms block. The present front door is very probably in the same place as the original entrance, and there is evidence to suggest there may have been a jetty right across the front.

(*right*) How the original jettied house is contained within the brick 'case'.

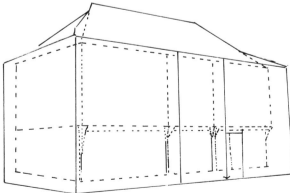

A further act for the suppression of the chantries in 1548 does list the properties in more detail, including 'one tenement with separate Chambers for two priests . . . situate and lying in the Churchyard of Horsham' and 'two small tenements adjoining to the same in the said Churchyard'. Of these tenements it is recorded that they were 'ever used by the Wardenis and Brotherne to be let to the poore wtoute anie rente taking for the same' . . . an early example of co-operative almshouses. Until about 1890, there were a number of medieval buildings in the Normandy at the east end of the church, including one called the Priests' House, and a row of cottages. These were first replaced as almshouses in 1884, and then demolished when the present buildings were renovated in the 1930s, and were almost certainly the 'normandy howses' which feature prominently in the churchwardens' accounts of the early 17th century. They appear to have included the tenements and priests' rooms associated with the parish gild, which were taken over by the parish after the dissolution.

These houses involved the parish in some considerable expense over the years 1610 to 1642 (the period of the incumbency of the Rev. John Collins) for renovation and general repairs. The three years of heaviest spending — 1619, 1624, and 1625 — are worth looking at in some detail for the light they throw on the nature of construction and upkeep of such buildings.

1619

Item payd to Thomas Tanner for the building of the new house in the normandye	£vii	xiid
Item paid to William Deane for laying in of the sells of the normandye houses	xiiis	iiiid
Item paid to John Ungley and William Rowland for masons work about the Normandye	xxis	xd
Item paid to John Foyce for careing of five loades of Pining stone	vs	
Item paid to him for careing of four loads of earth for the normandy howses	iis	
Item paid to John Dearling for the sawing of sells for the howses	vs	
Item paid to Nicholas Michell for five loades of pining stone	iis	vid

---

The sum of £7 1s. may have included some of the timber for the house, although three items concerning wood and cartage appear during the year's accounts and are probably part of the same job:

Item payd to Henry Fiest for 800 lathes at 12d the hundred	viiis	
Item payd to William Lintott for 3c of lathes	iis	vid
Item payd to William Deane for a dayes work loading of Timber		xiid

The relationship between the cost of this new house and the day's wage paid to William Deane is interesting — for him it represented 200 days' work, without allowing for any other outgoings at all. From other references it is possible to find out that John Joanes and his boy were paid 8s. for seven and a half days paving around the church in 1627, but by 1642, when he and his son spent five days on the same task, they only got five shillings. His labourer, John Stephens, was paid 4s. for giving three days' help in 1627, but a servant was only paid 5s. for giving six days' help in 1642. In the same year Robert Nye was paid 18d. for a day's carpentry, but the real aristocrat of workmen at the time seems to have been the 'stone healer' or roofer, such as James Michell, who received 25s. for eight days' work. As early as 1425 there is a record of a Horsham 'sclatter', William Brooker, being employed on roofing the hall of the Drapers' Guild in London, and even by this period, the 'stone healer' was able to command at least twice as much as a general mason or carpenter.

The expenses of the almshouses in 1624 and 1625 are all devoted to repair work — replacing wattle and daub, making and fixing new doors, repairing the stone roofs and the brick nogging and footings. From the materials used and the evidence of photographs, it is clear that these houses were standard timber-frame, with wattle-and-daub infill partly being replaced with small handmade bricks. There is a mention of wooden 'sells', which may well have been the horizontal ties at ground level into which the principal posts were pegged.

One more house in the Causeway may have been associated with the gild or one of the chantry endowments, but not as a house. The 'londes of the Fraternyte of Seynt John & Seynt Anne' appear under South Street in 1524–5, taxed at £8 on yearly value, so it may be that they also had some agricultural holdings, stretching back to the line of the present Worthing Road. The Chantry, next to Flagstones, looks too high for a medieval *house*, and so it is, for investigation has shown it to contain three bays of what must have been a *barn*. The crown-posts are massive, but crude, and totally clean. The bay to the north was probably added when the barn was converted to a house, possibly during the 17th century, when agricultural land so close to the centre was no longer feasible, or following the dissolution. The roof of the southern rear extension contains re-used timbers, including the top and bottom of a wooden mullioned window! In the 18th century, from at least 1705 until 1821, the house was called Causeway House, so the present name is rather a red herring. The chantry certificates do refer to a tenement called 'the chauntriehouse' with a barn, orchard, garden and one acre, but because of the later evidence it does not seem to be this property.

101. Normandy from west end of the cul-de-sac: pre-1890, showing Priests' House with shadow across its roof, and adjacent cottages at right angles, also 1844 almshouses (left foreground).

102. Normandy, east end of churchyard: rear of low, medieval Priests' House, and the weather-boarded cottages adjacent.

103. Normandy, from west end of cul-de-sac: post 1890, showing original almshouse cottages *after* the Priests' House was demolished.

Normandy, Horsham

104. *(left)* Normandy, east end of the churchyard. After demolition of the Priests' House, the weatherboarding was removed to reveal close-studding on adjacent cottages, very similar to the front of Bishops in Denne Road.

105. *(above)* Chantry, Causeway, 1985, showing 18th-century brick front.

(right) Diagram of barn within house.

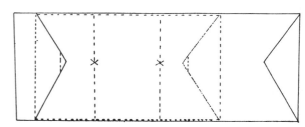

106. *(below)* Drawing of the Chantry.

BOLTERS, OR 15-16 CAUSEWAY

When John Michell, who lived in the 'Mancion Place at Stammerham' (now part of Christ's Hospital School), died in 1522, he was also in possession of Thetchers at Warnham (now Geerings), Field Place, Cockmannyscroft (where Park House now stands) and Bolters. His eldest son, Richard, inherited Field Place, his second son, John, added Thetchers to Hills Place, and his third son, Henry, got Cokmannys and Bolters. At this time, the latter cannot have been much more than the medieval 'tenement' which is mentioned in property transfers in the Causeway in 1425, 1437 and 1503. It had taken its name from the family who were owners at the two earliest dates, the Bolters — Thomas Bolter having been a Horsham representative at the parliaments of 1402 (at Westminster) and 1407 (in Gloucester). Three bays of this early hall-house still remain, running back at right angles from the present front range.

Changes of ownership are often marked by additions or alterations to houses, and Bolters is certainly a case in point. Soon after inheriting in 1522, Henry Michell must have decided to rebuild on a grand scale, although he left the crown-posted bays at the back, probably to serve as kitchens for his grand new house. We do not know whether the present frontage of 15-16 replaced a medieval range, or filled a space, but it seems to repeat a pattern of later frontages on early buildings at right angles, set farther back — such as to the east of the Town Hall, and in Causeway House (the Museum).

From examining this building it is possible to get some idea of what it must have been like; five bays long, jettied front and back, it had a four-flue chimney in the fourth bay, serving four hearths. Two of the chimney-pieces with their four-centred Tudor arches still exist, and the tall brick chimney towers above the roof. It is quite likely that the timber-framing on the front consisted of the regular vertical timbers called close-studding, which can be seen on a near-by building (no. 12), and it would have presented a most imposing frontage. No wonder Henry Michell was assessed at £20 under South Street residents in the 1524-5 subsidy! Although the new Bolters was still framed with heavy medieval-style timbers, it had built-in hearths, and was floored throughout, doing away with the old-fashioned smoke-filled open hall, and had a new style roof with queen struts, side purlins and wind-bracing. At that date, this construction was only well-known in the houses of the nobility and the lords of the Church. The upper chambers were so spacious and imposing, with their chamfered timbers, that it was quite easy to gain an extra storey at some time in the 17th century, by inserting a floor and two gable windows in the roof. By 1574, the house had been bought by Peter Ravenscroft, who left it in his will of that year to his son John, whose wife was an Elizabeth Michell.

In 1703, a conveyance shows that it had become Tredcroft property:

1/03 (1st & 2nd Oct.

Conveyance by Lease & Release, *Nathaniel Tredcroft*, of the Middle Temple, gent, to *Robert Hurst*, tailor

All that part of the *messuage formerly called BOLTERS*, lately called the Six Bells, barn, backside, garden and outhouse, now divided with pales and partitions from the orchard garden and the other part of the said mess. now in the possession of Nathaniel Tredcroft, with the gatehouse & gateway as far as it is divided with posts and rails within 12 inches breadth of the corner of the garden of John Parkhurst near the pond of the said Nathanial Tredcroft in the other part of the said way leading to a lane called Friday Lane from the South Street With free liberty to Robert Hurst to go & return with carts & carriages out of to and from Friday Lane in & through that part of the lane not granted to Robert Hurst to the premises granted to him

Which mess. is in South Street between the now dwellinghouse of the said John Parkhurst formerly an almshouse on the North side and the now dwellinghouse of Nathanial Tredcroft on the South side.

The messuage with the other part formerly belonging thereto and now belonging to Nat. Tredcroft were lately in possession of Amey Burnell, widow, or her under tenants and were lately granted to Thos. Delves of Eardshaw, Chester to Nat. Tredcroft. Cons. £150 6d. Quit rent to be paid to the Manor of Hewells.

Nathaniel Tredcroft's father, another Nathaniel, had been vicar of Horsham until he died in 1696. Presented to the living by Oliver Cromwell, which may say something about his churchmanship, he was at one time rated as one of the wealthiest men in Horsham. The family had steadily improved their lot from Thomas the tailor in the 1550s, through Robert the innkeeper (the *Red Lion* was on the site now occupied by Chart & Lawrence), Robert the vintner (who may have bought the fine Michell house), Nathaniel the wealthy cleric to Nathaniel of the Middle Temple, 'gent'. He married an heiress in 1702, and in 1703-4 built a new house in the very latest style — in brick and stone — just opposite the old family home. That was the original building that was called the Manor House, or Mr. Tredcroft's. Bolters was divided up, part going to another rising family, the Hursts, and presumably it was about this time that its timber-framed character was finally concealed behind 'modern' brick frontages.

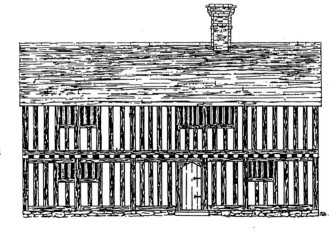

107. Bolters, as it probably appeared *c.* 1560.

108.   Bolters, or 15-16 Causeway.

The two original Tudor fireplaces remaining:
109.   Causeway, no. 15, ground floor.
110.   Causeway, no. 16, first floor.

111. *(left)* One of the queen strut bay-divisions, note lath and plaster infill.

12. *(right)* Ceiling joists in no. 16 show the line of the girder, beyond which projected the original front jetty, now concealed in the brick acade. The rear jetty is evident above a staircase in no. 15.

13. *(below left)* Some of the close-studding revealed in no. 16.

14. *(below right)* Plan and elevation of 15-16 Causeway.

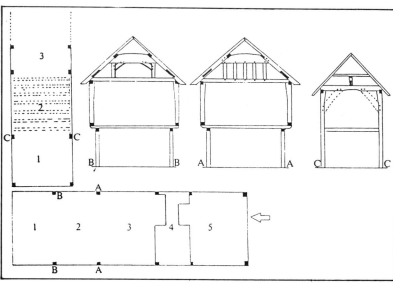

EAST STREET

Although I believe that East Street has grown out of an early alleyway leading from one of the north–south roads through Horsham to the market-place, the burgages which ran along each side had been developed in smaller portions by the 15th century at least, and with houses that faced onto the alley or street. From a photograph taken for a 1912 trade magazine, it is clear that there was a hall house with one cross-wing, probably jettied, on the site of what is now Wakefield's china shop, and was then Fawn's. Further east is the remains of yet another such house, until recently the fish-mongers', Leach Bros., but now acquired by the adjacent restaurant and painted to look like part of that building. As early photographs show, it was once a jettied cross-wing to a hall house that ran eastwards, and it may well be that a portion of the hall still remains to be recorded. From the way in which Luxford's building (Corn Factor and Seedsman) is butted up, it is quite probable that there was another eastern cross-wing, especially when one remembers that this house plan was characteristic of several of Horsham's medieval houses. At the end of 1985, the three-bay cross-wing to yet another hall-house was discovered within Nos. 13–15, between Wakefields and Leach Bros.

There is a considerable collection of deeds dating from 1566, on a house and garden in East Street called Vigours Mead. Only recently I came across a record of 1341, which concerned lands, rents and one house in Horsham belonging to the abbot of Fecamp, whose bailiff was a monk called Vigor. At that time they were rented for four shillings a year by Robert atte Herst. This kind of evidence suggests the existence, very early, of some kind of medieval house in East Street, and if it belonged to the church, the house was probably quite substantial.

By 1524-5, there were 13 men living in East Street (which may have included parts of Denne Road and Park Street) who were sufficiently well-off to be taxed, two of them at over ten pounds. Richard Ive, who died in 1531, also owned Randolfs or Randalls, a house and garden in West Street, which he left to his wife, Elizabeth, and there were two fullers and a pinner, who employed two servants. The other nine listed were all day labourers, one of whom had become a glover before he died in 1556. By the 1540s, it is recorded that Richard Mychell owned a brewhouse called Barwiks in East Street — a forerunner of King & Barnes? There are still several low timber-framed houses in East Street, but they are mainly 17th-century replacements or infill.

115.   Nos. 2 & 3 East Street in 1912, almost certainly another example of a hall-house with a jettied cross-wing. Only the ground line of the frontage of the modern building (below) reminds us of what has gone. The early photograph is an invaluable 'chance' record.

116.   Nos. 2 & 3 East Street in 1984.

117. Known for years as 'Leach's', after the fishmongers who occupied it, this has recently (1984) been absorbed by the restaurant now in Garner's, and the outside painted to appear as part of it. Actually, it was the jettied cross-wing to a hall house which extended in the direction of the Chinese 'take-away', which may possibly contain some of the old roof.

118. *(right)* This shows the framing for a window in the upstairs front corner of the west side of the cross-wing, through which someone could have looked right up to Middle Street.

119. *(below)* An early view of the building shows the hall range, part of which may remain, and inserted chimney. The 19th·century building (rt) may have replaced another cross-wing. The window (behind the street lamp) is still there. (*see* plate 117).

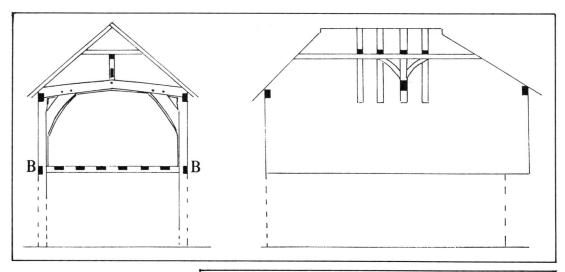

120. *(above)* Plan and elevation of Leach Bros., no. 4 East Street.

121. *(right)* Plan and elevation of no. 5 East Street.

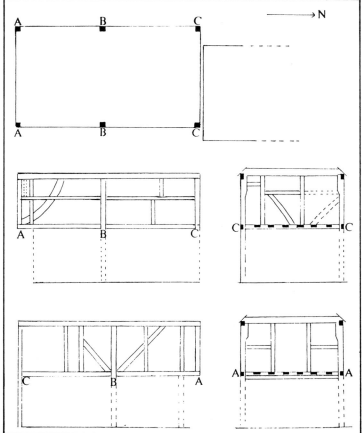

BISHOPRIC—MARLPOST

This street has had a variety of names — Oxford Road, 'the way to Guildford', and 'The Rookery' — within the last few hundred years, and its modern name is slightly inaccurate. It should more properly be called '*Arch*bishopric', as this is a reminder that once this marked the beginning of the Archbishop of Canterbury's land, Marlpost, which was an outlier of the manor of Tarring, where he had one of his palaces. Marlpost seems to have covered much of the area out towards Broadbridge Heath, and up Tower Hill, along Two Mile Ash at the back of Southwater. It was then a heavily wooded area, as one of the earliest surviving 'custumals' (or record of manorial dues and customs) dating from about 1290, reminds us — the 26 tenants had to provide 10 loads of firewood or charcoal for the parent manor each year. They also sent wheat, corn, oats and barley, so some of the area was already cleared and cultivated to some purpose. Three of the tenants, Alice, Robert and Julian, are described as being 'at Holebroke', and there was already a Patching, a Snelling, and a Pilfold. Because this was an outlier, it needed a beadle to see that everything was running according to the laws of the manor, and to report to Tarring four times a year. For these duties he was allowed 8d. off his rent, food or a penny each time he visited Tarring; he could run two of his animals with the lord's; have five pigs on the 'mast' in the lord's wood; and take the roots of fallen trees and five cartloads of fallen branches. It is quite likely that a special house was provided at some time for the beadle, and where the lord or his representative could lodge on visits to the outlier, or where manorial courts could be held. This would have been even more necessary after 1449, when the archbishop was granted the right to hold a weekly market and two annual fairs here, probably to 'cash-in' on the success of Horsham Borough.

The manor court was held at the *Green Dragon*, in Bishopric, in 1779, and it is possible that this house had an earlier connection with the administration of the manor. It is an early hall house, with two cross-wings, and both the crown-post on the open tie over the hall and that in the eastern cross-wing, are finely finished. The house was possibly jettied at the front, and when a chimney was put in, it was fortunately housed in the small hall bay behind the open tie, leaving the crown-post intact. The decoration of crown-posts, one in an upper chamber, and the size and quality of the timber, suggest ecclesiastical origins, so perhaps this was put up when the market and fairs increased the administration of the manor, or possibly earlier.

Only yards away from the *Green Dragon*, to the west, is a house that could repay further investigation. Some timbering is still visible in a side wall to the rear, seen through the gates of King & Barnes Brewery, and the large rendered chimney is so clearly an early brick stack hidden behind later facing. The façade, too, with its bay windows, looks like a later attempt at 'up-dating', in time-honoured fashion.

'They had a long life — but they went almost overnight': so read a headline in the *West Sussex County Times* in 1970, when another row of old cottages in the Bishopric were demolished. One had been the birthplace of one of Horsham's colourful residents of the 19th century — Henry Burstow — whose 'reminiscences' were recorded and published by William Albery in 1911. Burstow had lived there for 42 years, from 1826, and described it as 'one common living room eleven feet square, about six foot six high, opening on to the street, and a kitchen and scullery on the ground floor; upstairs were three small bedrooms'. *The Jolly Ploughboy* inn had also been part of the range, just a few yards from the *King's Arms*, which was certainly an inn by 1667, and from its construction was probably not built much more than seventy years earlier. It was only when the last group of cottages were being demolished, that it became clear that they were very early — although a photograph shows that the evidence was quite visible. Fortunately they were measured and drawn before they were flattened, proving to be a 'continuous jetty' type, almost certainly used as combined homes, workshops and shop premises. It may be that the small range which still exists to the west of the *King's Arms* is of a similar type — it is to be hoped that they too can be recorded, if not conserved. That there were these kinds of buildings before 1550 in this area, proves that trading had spread beyond the bounds of the borough by an early date.

Just down the Worthing Road from the modern Tesco store, south of the burial ground in front of the Free Church, is a small low building, extended at the rear, with a hipped roof. A visit has confirmed that this is just two bays of a medieval house — the floored end bay of either solar or service, and one bay of a hall — apparently another survivor of the manor of Marlpost, just outside the borough boundary. There is a property indenture of 1789 which describes the cottages to the south of this house as 'new erected' so by this date the rest of the hall house had been demolished — another hall bay and at least one more floored bay. It was then in the hands of the Rowland family, who were leading lights in the Anabaptist community who had established the Horsham Free Church. In 1411 John Newdegate made a grant to Henry Boteler of Horsham (of Butler's Chantry) of a dovecote in the garden of a tenement at Lynde next to Lyndecrouche in Horsham; even in the 1789 indenture, the Worthing road is variously described as 'Tanbridge Lane' or 'the way leading from Lynn Cross to Tanbridge', and Lynn Cross was an early name for the cross roads where there is now a one-way system and an underpass, at the top of the Bishopric. Perhaps the dovecote was in the garden of the hall house that has partially survived.

A prestigious and more complete survival within the boundaries of the Archbishop's manor, just tucked away on Blackbridge Lane, near its junction with the Worthing Road, is Netherledys. This is Horsham's third surviving 'wealden', with recessed hall and jettied wings like 19-20 Causeway and 26-28 Carfax, and most certainly the grandest. A chimney was inserted into the single-bay open hall in the 16th century, and it still retains a fine heavily moulded dais beam with the original post and plank screen beneath and the original doorhead over the door leading to the floored solar end. This doorhead is matched by those over the doors in the service end, where there was a cross-passage, screened from the hall with another planking screen — a fragment still exists under yet another moulded beam. This is the only local house to have *two* such beams, although this feature is common in the East Sussex–Kent areas.

This very fine example of the wealden type, possibly built at the end of the 14th century, was put at right-angles to what appears to be an earlier, much cruder building, which then became the kitchen quarters. In 1487, the tenant of Netherledys, or 'the farm belonging to Netherled' — one possible derivation — was William Ryprost, who died leaving it to his widow, Joanna, according to the Marlpost court roll. By the end of the 16th century it had passed into the hands of the Monk family, who were related to the Michells of Cuckfield.

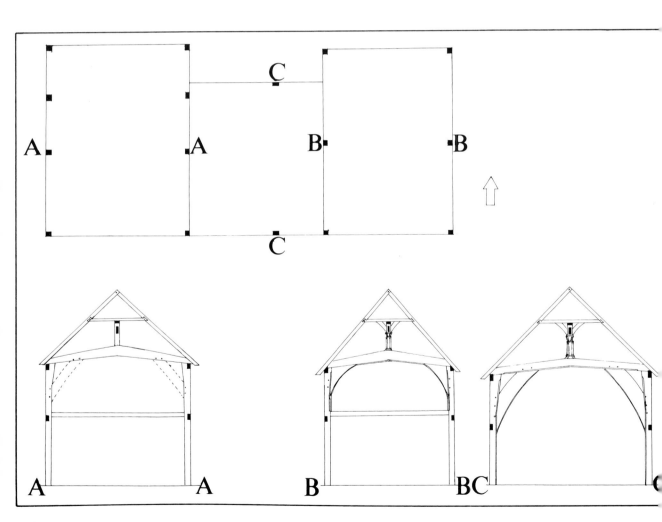

122.   Plan and elevation of *The Green Dragon*.

123. *The Green Dragon,* Bishopric. Remains of timbering can be seen in the side wall, and possible evidence for an underbuilt jetty. The tile-hanging now covers the rest of the upper floor timbering.

124. The crown post that stood over the open hall, now on the chimney breast. Note the roll moulding at top and base.

125. The end wall of the hall (facing picture above). The horizontal timber serves both for the end tie of the hall and eave-plate for the western cross-wing.

126. *(left)* One of the braces to the tie over the open hall. The modern light bulb gives some idea of scale! The smaller framing was inserted with the chimney when the hall was floored.

127. *(above)* The crown-post on the tie over the upper chamber in the eastern cross-wing. This chamber may have served an official function for the lodging of the representative of the lord of the manor (the Archbishop of Canterbury) or for holding manorial rent collections or courts.

128. *(below)* Another survivor from the 16th century.

129. The *King's Arms* in the Bishopric: an
early photograph shows *two* small ranges of
cottages to the right of the 17th-century inn.

130. This modern view shows the parade of
shops that has replaced the old cottages.

131. By the 1960s, the range next to the *Kings Arms* had gone, revealing clearly the medieval crown-posting and bracing. Nevertheless, this was demolished also in 1970, and was then found to have been a row of medieval jettied shops, with decorative Elizabethan painting on some of the timbers.

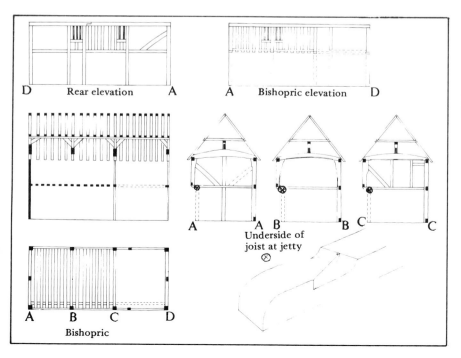

132. Plan and elevation of 38, 40, 42 Bishopric, Horsham.

133. A cottage in Worthing Road which contains
two bays of a hall house; a floored end and one
bay of the hall. (*right*) Diagram showing a
floored end and one bay of the hall.

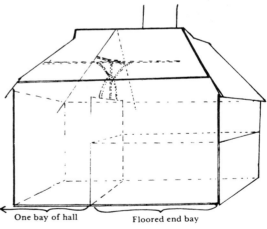

One bay of hall   Floored end bay

134. The partition crown-post (ie. with down
braces) that marks the end of a hall.

135. Netherledys before division into two dwellings.

136. Plan of Netherledys house and site.

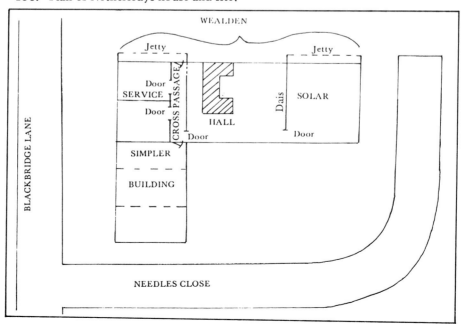

137. Crown-post on partition at south end of hall, above dais beam and screen.

138. Crenellated dais beam above planked screen at south end of hall. The moulded girder (centre) and chamfered and stopped joists are all part of the inserted floor — late 16th/ early 17th century. Notice original doorhead to the right.

139. Corner assembly, south-west corner, showing principal post, end-tie, eave-plate and down-brace. (See sketch)

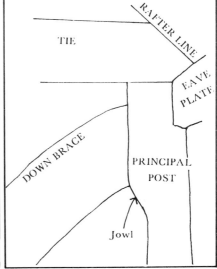

K-SHOE SHOP, CARFAX

A combination of evidence has established the existence of another hall-house with two cross-wings, right in the middle of what was the open market-place. The part of the house that still exists seems to be the eastern cross-wing, the upper part of which is easily seen by paying a visit to the men's department of the shoe shop upstairs. There, above head-height, is the open tie that would have spanned the upper chamber, supporting a finely-chamfered crown-post, with moulded cap and base, braced four ways to purlin and collars, and behind, the crown-post with down-braces, which marked a partition or end-wall.

Drawings of the buildings on the centre island of the Carfax, executed about 1840 by Thomas Mann, and reproduced in William Albery's *Millenium*, show a building adjacent to the west side of this cross-wing, even then encased in the early 19th-century building. Once Clark's the fishmongers, this western range is very clearly a hall and one cross-wing, and was drawn even more precisely in 1879, in such a way as to suggest that it was once all of a piece with the section in the shoe shop. The Mann drawing which shows the eastern side of the island suggests the existence of yet another hall-house with one cross-wing, so it seems that this centre was already built-up by an early date in the town's history — by the mid-15th century — as this area was in theory open 'waste', common to all.

The 1524–5 subsidy lists record three people living in 'The Skarfolkes', who might have been wealthy enough to have owned a house of the quality suggested by the remaining fragment — Rychard Busshop, Thomas Elys, and Rychard Sharpe. From the will of Richard Bishop, the elder, who died in 1544, it is clear that he owned a 'howse and garden in the borowghe of Horsham', although by that date it was being rented to Thomas Sayer. He also owned lands and tenements in Ifield, Charlwood, Rusper and Cuckfield, apart from other land in Horsham parish and a stable and yard in West Street. These were distributed among his wife and three children, John (who died an infant), Alice, of whom he seemed particularly fond and who later married a servant in the house of the Earl of Arundel, and Richard, who married Elisabeth Voyce. From the younger Richard's will (he died ten years later), the family then owned lands in Cuckfield and a number of properties in Horsham — a house and three gardens in North Street (once in the tenure of Richard Sharpe) a house and three gardens called Manncells in West Street, property in Friday Lane or Back Lane, once Rapkyns, 'three crofts lying at Wimbelpost called Holbrooks', and *a house and garden in the market place* of Horsham. Richard Bishop, the younger, had four children — three daughters and a son, Thomas, who died aged thirteen. The house in the market place was willed to the eldest daughter, another Elizabeth, just like her mother and grandmother.

Looking at the Bishop family tree, just father and son, it is interesting to notice one or two details or 'coincidences' that must have given fuel for gossip in the Horsham of the day. After the death of Richard the elder, his wife married William Warren, who was in service to the Countess of Arundel, and it must have been through her that her daughter, Alice, met *her* husband, Richard Ryckman, who served the Earl. At that time Chesworth House was still frequently used by the Norfolk family, so the servants to the household would have been familiar faces in Horsham. Richard the younger had married a Voyce, whose father, Henry, is mentioned in the will of the elder Bishop. This Elizabeth had a daughter, Margaret, after her husband's death, who could have been a posthumous child, but three years later she bore a bastard son to Thomas Bradbridge, a member of another well-known Horsham family, who was one of the witnesses to her husband's will! We can only wonder what the aunt thought of this piece of errant behaviour!

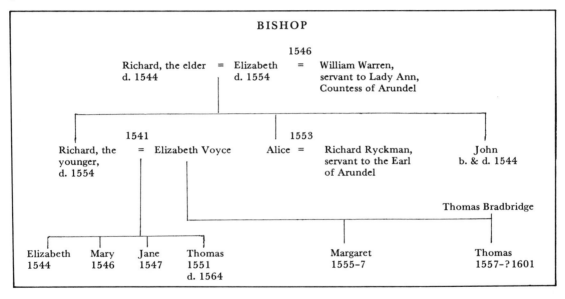

140.   The Bishop family tree.

141. A more accurate drawing by Henry Burstow
of the hall and cross-wing shown by Thomas Mann
The right-hand end suggests some alteration or los

142. This modern view from the east shows that the K-Shoe shop building existed when Thomas Mann
executed his drawing, and that part of it must have adjoined the building also drawn by Burstow.

163. The jowled post and corner assembly are clear evidence of a timber-framed building parallel to the street. The eave-plate continues over two bay lengths.

164. This 18th-century school board was in use for flooring. It rests against the remains of partition framing.

CHESWORTH HOUSE

Historically the most important house in Horsham must be that at Chesworth, on the north bank of the river Arun, east of the parish church. The name itself is a reminder of the Saxon origins of the town — Ceoldred's worth, or Ceoldred's farm — and it was almost certainly included in the lands belonging to the parent manor of Washington, that was granted to the first William de Braose by William the Conqueror. Because the development of the site is inextricably linked with the fortunes of the several families involved, and even with national events, I must try to give a brief sketch of the relevant history.

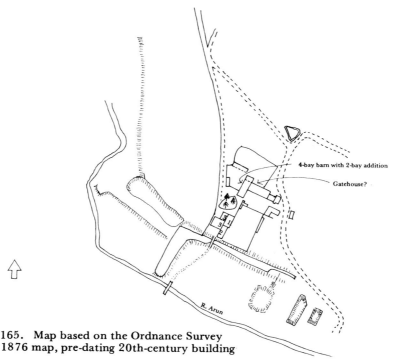

165. Map based on the Ordnance Survey
1876 map, pre-dating 20th-century building

In 1232, at the age of 12, the fourth William to inherit succeeded his father, John, who had been killed in a fall from his horse while riding near Bramber. Both this William, when he came of age, and his son, the fifth William de Braose, seemed to spend much of their time going to law over various parts of their property, more often than not with members of their own family. Their problems really arose because of the extent of the de Braose holdings, and the complicated relationships from re-marriages.

William (IV), who died in 1290, was involved in a lengthy case with his half-sister, Matilda Giffard (previously married to William Longespey, earl of Salisbury), who may have been at Chesworth in 1271, when a 'Matilda de perco' — 'of the park' — was recorded living in the parish. William himself was granted free warren in Chesworth park by the king only ten years later. He married three times, having children by each wife, and so storing up trouble for his son and heir, the fifth William. It was the third wife, and widow, Mary de Roos, whom this fifth William was called to meet in June, 1292, at Horsham, when they were to come to some arrangement over a part of the inheritance which included Chesworth. By 1326, when William died, Chesworth was in the hands of Thomas, son of his half-brother, Peter, one of Mary's sons.

When English kings moved about the country, they headed any administrative papers with the place where they were staying at the time, so we know that Edward II stayed at Chesworth for a few days in 1324, and it is possible that it was also one of the Horsham houses that Edward I stayed at in 1299, although some papers are headed 'at Holebrook'. In both cases, the kings and their retinue would have been the guests of William (V), who provided men, money and leadership for the Welsh campaigns, as befitted a Marcher lord.

By 1506, the de Braose line had died out and title passed through females and the Mowbrays into the Howard family, who had been given the dukedom of Norfolk under Richard III. The third duke certainly spent some time at Chesworth, before he succeeded his father in 1524, and his mother chose to live there as dowager. This duchess was grandmother to both Ann Boleyn and Catherine Howard (who may even have stayed at Horsham), and the echoes of their tragic careers must have been heard in the town, especially as crown agents were sent to shut up the house, when the old lady was summoned to her grand-daughter Catherine's trial in 1542. A great-grand-daughter, Elizabeth, was christened in the parish church in 1543, so one of the duke's younger sons had moved into his grandmother's house.

The next family disaster, arising out of hatred of the Howards by other aspiring courtiers, was centred around the heir to the ducal crown — the Earl of Surrey — son of the third duke, father of the fourth, and cousin to both the ill-fated queens. He was beheaded for treason in 1547, and the old duke only survived in prison because of the death of the king, Henry VIII. Only a few years before, after his niece's affair, he had retired to the house at Chesworth for the winter. Now all the family homes were forfeit, including Chesworth, and were ransacked by crown agents taking inventories. However, with the accession of Mary after her brother's death in 1553, the Howards were restored to favour, though not at once to all their property, and the old duke was released, to die a year later.

In 1555 the new duke (another Thomas) still only 17, married Mary Fitzalan, daughter of the Earl of Arundel. She died just three years later, giving birth to the son who was to become both Duke of Norfolk and Earl of Arundel. It may have been that the Earl of Arundel and his family, as Lord Steward of the royal household, had been able to use Chesworth as a small family home, for between 1545 and 1558 there are numerous entries in the parish registers concerning members of the Arundel household. Mary herself may have spent time there, and certainly her father, the old Earl, and brother-in-law, John Lord Lumley, must have been staying there a month after her death in London, when they stood as godfathers to the son of John Apsley of Stammerham.

Horsham was one of 11 boroughs in the Duke's patronage — five in Norfolk and six in Sussex — and often Norfolk men were returned for the Sussex boroughs, such as Richard Fulmerston and John Blennerhasset in 1558. The same Blennerhasset was one of the lessees of Chesworth in 1572, when the house had seen its last real excitement in its long history: the fourth duke had reached too high, aspiring to put Mary, Queen of Scots, on the English throne, and possibly to marry her himself, restoring a Catholic monarchy. He was arrested, tried, and executed for high treason, and Chesworth was never again part of the Norfolk holdings, deteriorating through a succession of tenancies, in Crown ownership, until the 20th century.

Between 1577 and 1582, one of the tenants was Bishop Curtis of Chichester, who may have spent some time there, as there is a reference in the parish registers to 'my lord of Chichester's capell at Chisworth' where one of his clerks, Jeremy Cooke, married a local girl, and their daughter was born, and possibly baptised there, at Chesworth, in 1584. An inventory of the bishop's goods, taken after his death in 1582, mentions that Mrs. Curtis still held the lease, and lists a number of animals and farm equipment, as well as furnishings and utensils in parlour, kitchen and milkhouse. James Allen, then the master at Collyer's, who was also the local notary, made a declaration that he had been asked by Mrs. Curtis to remove the bedding, as two doors at the house had been broken open. Vandals seem to have been a problem even then!

What remains at the Chesworth site, though substantial, must only be a fraction of the complex of buildings that must have been there from an early date. Embedded in the main part of the present house are the visible remains of the principal timbers of three bays of a very large, medieval, open-hall house, at least 26 feet wide, which almost certainly extended further to the north. Although the roof was replaced when the hall was floored, probably in the second half of the 16th century, there is some evidence of crown-posting left on one tie. There is not nearly enough to say that this was part of the house that Edward II stayed in, but it must have been of this kind and quality on this site. This was certainly part of the 'hall' mentioned in an inventory taken in 1549, when the house had been briefly in the hands of Edward Seymour, who was attaindered in that year. It is also quite possible that the 'great chamber, dining chamber and chapel', also mentioned in that inventory, may have been located within the brick range that still stands to the south of the original hall. A private chapel at such a house need never have been more than a small room, particularly as residents seem to have made use of the parish church. Some 20 other rooms are itemised in this inventory, some hung with tapestries, as well as other offices, so the complex must have covered much of the site that is now given over to the farm and its buildings. There are fragments of what may have been courtyard walls incorporated into present boundary walls, and a large contemporary barn, originally of four bays, close-studded at the northern end, which with the adjacent building may have formed the gatehouse group, mentioned in the 1650 parliamentary survey. By 1650, the ranges to the west of the old hall were probably built, replacing some of the other buildings which had fallen into disrepair and become uninhabitable to the point of demolition. The brick range that remains is possibly the remnant of work carried out by the third duke of Norfolk, who built the family's chief residence at Kenninghall, when he succeeded his father in 1524. Once described as 'a fine residence of ornamental brick-work', not a stone remains of that house.

166 & 167.   The northern side of Chesworth. The left-hand range contains the remains of the open-hall, which extended to the north. The parallel range and that at right angles were added later, possibly in the 17th century.

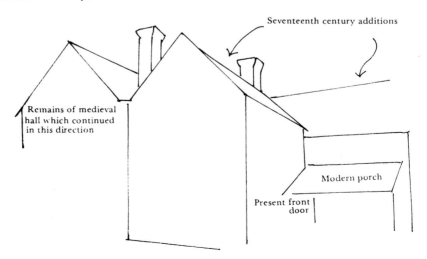

Seventeenth century additions

Remains of medieval hall which continued in this direction

Modern porch

Present front door

168.   The Tudor brick range at the rear (south) of the medieval hall. The moulded brick treatment generally denotes building quality. This range was probably higher, judging by the gable end of the hall, which could explain references to the Earl of Surrey's 'tower', in inventories. The range possibly contained the chapel, and at least one other important chamber.

169.   One of the large principal posts in the earliest range, with an empty mortice for an up-brace to the tie, which has a corresponding empty mortice.

170.   One of the remaining up-braces for an open tie, still in position in the early range.

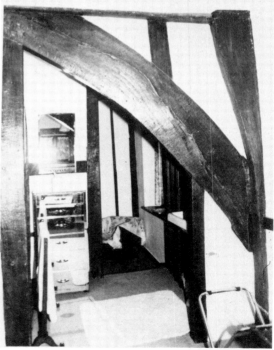

BIBLIOGRAPHY

Local

Albery, W., *A Parliamentary History of Horsham* (1927)
—   *A Millenium of facts about Horsham and Sussex* (1947)
Armstrong, J. R., *A History of Sussex* (1978)
Booker, J. M. L. (ed.) *The Wiston Archives* (1975)
Brandon, P., *The Sussex Landscape* (1974)
—   (ed.) *The South Saxons* (1978)
Burstow, H., *Reminiscences of Horsham* (1911)
Elwes, D. G. C., *The Family of De Braose, 1066-1326* (1883)
Hurst, D., *The History and Antiquities of Horsham*, 2nd edn. (1889)
Mason, R., *Framed Buildings of the Weald*, 2nd edn. (1969)
Salzman, L., *The Chartulary of Sele Priory* (1923)
Windrum, A. H., *Horsham: An historical survey* (1977)
Willson, A. N., *A History of Collyer's School, 1532-1964* (1965)
Steer, F. W. (ed.) *Arundel Castle Archives*, Vol. 1 (1968), Vol. 2 (1972)
Sussex Record Society:
    Vol. 2   Sussex Fines 1190-1248
    Vol. 3   Inquisitions Post Mortem 1558-83
    Vol. 7   Sussex Fines 1249-1307
    Vol. 10 Subsidy Rolls, 1296, 1327, 1332
    Vol. 14 Inquisitions Post Mortem 1485-1649
    Vol. 21 Horsham Parish Register, 1541-1635
    Vol. 23 Sussex Fines 1308-1509
    Vol. 36 Chantry Records
    Vol. 42 Transcripts of Sussex Wills (vol. 2)
Sussex Archaeological Collections: various volumes

General

Braun, H., *Parish Churches: Their Architectural Development in England* (1974)
Brunskill, R. W., *Illustrated Handbook of Vernacular Architecture* (1978)
Clark, P. and Slack, P., *English Towns in Transition 1500-1700* (1976)
Clifton-Taylor, A., *The Pattern of English Building* (1972)
Darby, H. C. and Campbell, E. M. J. (eds.) *The Domesday Geography of South-East England* (19
Darby, H. C. (ed.) *A New Historical Geography of England before 1600* (1976)
Foster, I. and Alcock, L. (eds.) *Culture & Environment* (1963)
Harris, R., *Discovering Timber-framed Buildings* (1981)
Hewett, C. A., *The Development of Carpentry, 1200-1700: An Essex Study* (1969)
Hunnisett, R. F., *The Mediaeval Coroner* (1961)
McKisack, M., *The Parliamentary Representation of English Boroughs in the Middle Ages* (1932)
Mason, R., *Framed Buildings of England* (1978)
Platt, C., *Mediaeval England* (1978)
—   *The English Mediaeval Town* (1979)
—   *Parish Churches of Mediaeval England* (1981)
Reynolds, S., *An Introduction to the History of English Mediaeval Towns* (1977)
Salzman, L. *English Industries of the Middle Ages* (1923)
—   *Building in England down to 1540* (1952)
Tate, W. E., *The Parish Chest* (1983)
Taylor, C., *Village And Farmstead* (1983)

INDEX OF PERSONS

INDEX OF HORSHAM PLACE-NAMES

Obsolete place-names are shown in brackets; alternative spellings or alternative names with a slash between them.

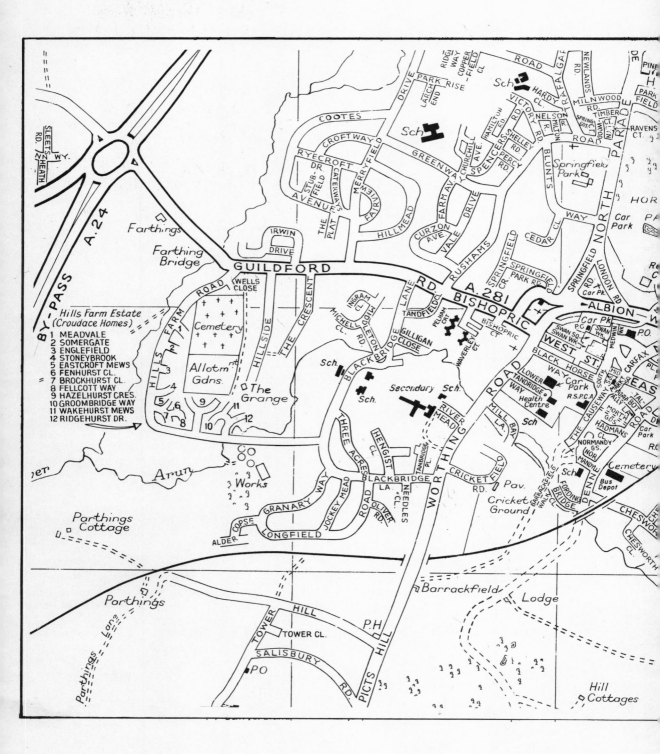